毕淑敏
双语美文

*A Bilingual Edition of
Beautiful Stories
by Bi Shumin*

U0725845

与美好相遇

Encountering Beauty

毕淑敏　著

朱虹　刘海明　译

GUANGXI NORMAL UNIVERSITY PRESS
广西师范大学出版社
·桂林·

与美好相遇

YU MEIHAO XIANGYU

出版统筹：张俊显
品牌总监：耿　磊
选题策划：耿　磊
责任编辑：王芝楠
助理编辑：韩杰文
美术编辑：卜翠红　刘冬敏
营销编辑：杜文心　钟小文
责任技编：李春林

图书在版编目（CIP）数据

与美好相遇：汉、英／毕淑敏著；朱虹，刘海明
译. —桂林：广西师范大学出版社，2020.1
　（毕淑敏双语美文）
　ISBN 978-7-5598-2393-9

Ⅰ.①与… Ⅱ.①毕…②朱…③刘… Ⅲ.①散文集—
中国—当代—汉、英 Ⅳ.①I267

中国版本图书馆 CIP 数据核字（2019）第 273112 号

广西师范大学出版社出版发行

（ 广西桂林市五里店路 9 号　邮政编码：541004 ）
　网址：http://www.bbtpress.com
出版人：黄轩庄
全国新华书店经销
保定市中画美凯印刷有限公司印刷
（保定市西三环 1566 号　邮政编码：071000）
开本：880 mm × 1 350 mm　1/32
印张：6　　字数：120 千字
2020 年 1 月第 1 版　　2020 年 1 月第 1 次印刷
印数：0 001~6 000 册　　定价：39.80 元

如发现印装质量问题，影响阅读，请与出版社发行部门联系调换。

在书中温暖相遇

几年前，广西师范大学出版社出版了我的一套书。在这套书里，我写了自己在遥远西藏的往事，写了当医生的难忘经历，写了担当心理医生时听到的故事和引发的思考……

书是缔造心灵的塑形工具。东方文化中，心并不单单指那个解剖学上的泵血器官，而是汇聚每个人的品格情操的智慧之海。有一颗仁慈之心，会爱世界爱他人爱生活，爱自身也爱大家。有一颗自强之心，会勤学苦练百折不挠，宠辱不惊大智若愚。有一颗尊严之心，会珍惜自然善待万物。有一颗流量充沛羽翼丰满的心，会乘上幻想飞船，抚摸众星的翅膀。

我遇到了朱虹老师，她就是拥有这样一颗多彩之心的睿智长者。很高兴她喜欢我书中的文字。

最初，朱虹老师想挑一些篇章翻译，作为礼物送给远在大洋彼岸的孙女外孙女们珍藏。广西师大出版社的编辑获悉这个想法，郑重邀请朱虹和刘海明老师，将本套书全部翻译出来。

这不是轻易可完成之事，是颇为繁复艰辛的工程。朱虹老师已年近90，是中国社科院德高望重的英美文学研究专家，也是一位把我国很多当代文学作品翻译介绍到国外的杰出翻译家。长期生活在国外的刘海明老师造诣高超文采斐然，和朱虹老师相得益彰珠联璧合。两位老师以醇厚学养和丰富经验，深思熟虑地将这些文字，按照英语思维方式和阅读风格，给予精彩转化，赋予它们以另外一种语言表达的鲜活生命。

补充一个小插曲。我的散文"精神的三间小屋"，被选入2018年教育部审定的全国义务教育语文教科书九年级上册。刘海明老师加班加点，将这篇文章翻译出来，收入本套书，真是雪中送炭。

面对这套双语书，我心中充盈知遇之恩和感念之情，在此向所有付出心血的老师们深表谢意！

人生是砥砺向前且充满顿挫的历程，不时筋疲力尽茫然四顾。这本小书的故事和它的成书过程，让我又一次相信，行程中有不期而至的风雨，更有美好温暖的巧遇。朱虹、海明老师和我在文字中结识，现在，我期待着——我们和你——亲爱的读者，在书中相逢。

之后，让咱们再次充满信心地出发！

2019年11月5日

When We Meet Inside a Book

A few years ago, Guangxi Normal University Press published a collection of my stories. In them, I wrote about the years I spent in remote Tibet, my unforgettable experience working as a physician, and stories and musings I gathered as a counseling psychologist.

Works of literature help shape our heart. In Eastern cultures, the heart is the sea of wisdom that nurtures our character, other than a mere organ anatomically responsible for pumping blood through the body. It is with the kind heart that one loves the world, others and life; love of oneself and all people. It is with the hardy, aspiring heart that one strives on, never giving up, and is wise, artless and unflappable. It is with the dignified heart that one cherishes nature and is kind to all creatures great and small. It is with the heart brimful of confidence that one floats on wings of imagination, touching the stars.

Then I met Zhu Hong, an erudite elder with such an unfailingly rich heart, and was most delighted that she liked the stories of this collection.

Initially, Zhu Hong had planned to translate a selection of them as a gift to be held dear by her granddaughters across the ocean. However, when the editorial staff of Guangxi Normal University Press learned about this, they decided to invite Zhu Hong and Liu Haiming to translate the entire collection into English.

It was no small undertaking, a project requiring much dedication. Zhu Hong, in her late eighties, is a venerated scholar in the field of English and American Literature with the Chinese Academy of Social Sciences. She is also noted for her incomparable translations of outstanding works of modern Chinese literature, bringing them to a wider international audience. Liu Haiming, an accomplished translator having studied and worked extensively abroad, collaborated with Zhu Hong on this project. The two scholar-translators pored over the Chinese texts and managed to bring out the spirit of the original, and give life to the stories in the English language in all its beauty and flexibility.

Incidentally, my essay "Three Little 'Rooms' for Your Soul" was selected for the 2018 edition of the Ministry of Education-approved high school textbook for Chinese Language and Literature, for the first semester of the ninth year of National Compulsory Education. Beavering away, Liu Haiming had it timely translated for inclusion in the present collection.

As this bilingual collection was ready for printing, I felt most grateful for our privileged connection. My thanks go to all who have put all the hard work into its publication.

Life is a journey, with inevitable challenges and setbacks, which, at times, can wear you out, and loneliness captures you. Yet, for all the storms out of the blue, there are also fortuitous, heartening encounters along the way—a belief borne out by the stories in this collection and its publication. Zhu Hong, Haiming and I met in the pages of these stories, and now I look forward to our encounter with you, dear readers, in this little collection.

Then, brimful of confidence again, we will journey on!

Bi Shumin, November 5, 2019

contents
目 录

contents
目　录

领悟人生的亮色

毕淑敏：

　　我是第一次接受女中学生的访问，心情激动。在你们提问之前，我先讲两句话：一是，我非常羡慕你们这个年龄。你们会说羡慕什么，我们还羡慕你们呢，可以独立自主，不必事事要听父母摆布。但这羡慕的话绝对是肺腑之言，因为一个人年轻的时候，那种蓬勃的生命力，那种开放的、多方面去锻炼成长、吸收知识、增长聪明才干的时光，不是人生的哪个阶段都能得到的，而这个阶段又是极短暂的，会飞快地逝去。因此，我希望你们珍惜中学时光。

另一句是，女生对世界的感觉往往比男生更细腻更敏感，她是用自己整个的身心去体验生活中的快乐与悲伤，感受成就与挫折，并将之折射进自己的心灵。女性心理上的这种独特性，决定女性时常是凭感情与直觉去把握事物，支配行为。这个世界不是到处都有鲜花，永远是春天，每天都是温暖的，有时会有阴天和冷天，会遇到艰难和曲折，这些对女孩子影响的分量也会更重。因此，女孩子要成就一番事业，一定要有坚强、坚定的意志，才有可能去领悟人生的亮色。

女学生：

谢谢您讲的肺腑之言。我们非常敬重您，喜欢您的作品，羡慕您的丰富经历。您的中学时代是怎样度过的？对您今日的成功有什么影响？

毕淑敏：

我中学就读于北京外语学院附中，校址就在现在的和平门中学内。三十年前学外语，尤其是从初中就专学外语是很时髦的，也是极难得的机会。考外院附中岂止是百里挑一，那是从四百个人中取一人，我幸运地考上了这所学校。这所学校很怪，男生比例特别大，大约要占百分之七十以上，记得我所在的班只有九个女生。那时，在中国男士的印象中，没有"女子优先"的意识，作为一个女孩，学习成绩必须特别优秀，否则班上没人重视你的存在。这是一种男女不平等的表现。尽管你们现在面对的世界比我们那时要好得多，但是也不会从天上掉下来一个男女完全平等的生存环境，女性要在世界上安身立命，只有靠自强自立。

就在我读初中时，学校却停课了。我从小就爱学习，各科成绩都不错，但心里仍惧怕考试，尤其是怕外籍老师的考试，因为外籍老师考的内容常常变幻莫测，随心所欲，无法预测。即使平时努力做好准备，考试时仍难对付。正当准备迎考时，突然宣布不上课，不考试了，怎么不让学生高兴呀。可是后来发现，终日聊天无所事事，没有知识的长进，才感到空虚和厌烦。

我的学校有一个很好的图书馆，当时图书馆有条特殊的规定，凡借看一本书，还书时必须交一篇特殊的稿件，否则就不能再借书。苛刻的条件没阻止我们读书的热情，我们几个女生一窝蜂地跑到图书馆，每人借回一本书，互相传看着。为了取得借书资格，我只好违心写上一篇符合图书馆要求的稿子。记得我当时读的是托尔斯泰的《战争与和平》，于是稿子里就写上：托尔斯泰的《战争与和平》宣扬了资产阶级人道主义，他的错误观念主要表现在如下段落，请见第五十页，下面我就挑上一段托尔斯泰的精彩语句；再见第一百四十五页，下面又是一段原文摘录，而且我抄写得还很工整。由于当时是如饥似渴地读了这些书，又很认真地做了记录，至今书中许多段落我还记忆犹新。就这样，我取得了图书馆老师的信任，用这种方法不断地借书——读书——还书。其他同学渐渐地懒得写文章，陆陆续续地不再去图书馆借书了，可是他们又想知道书中的内容，于是同宿舍的同学出了一个主意："让毕淑敏每天晚上给大家讲小说中的故事。"这样，就像长篇小说连续广播似的，我每天给大家讲上一小时，从未间断过。我讲过雨果的《笑面人》，听过我讲这篇小说的一位同学，现在在美国，她告诉我，听了我讲的之后，她就再不想看原著了，因为印象太深了。回想起来，同学们的这个主意，还真让我受益匪浅，因为我不仅要天天看书，还要认真读懂；不仅要记牢，而且要把故事完完整整地复述出来。在这两三年里，虽然停课了，可我却通过这种自学方式，读了大量名著，讲了许多故事，从而打好了文学功底，提高了语言表达能力。名著是前人以智慧的头脑把对人生的感悟、对世界的体验，用文字记载下来。它像一把火炬照亮人生、启迪后人，这是人类文明的传递，也是人自我完善的火种。

女学生：

听说您当过兵，做过军医，又在西藏阿里生活了十一年，您觉得这种生活的价值是什么？

毕淑敏：

我出生在一个军人家庭，如果说我的良好教养、善良品格受之于我的父母，那么成就我的事业、奠定我的人生价值的该是中国西部的阿里高原，是她在我心中留下了刻骨铭心的印记。

那是一九六八年底，冬季征兵开始。我当时确实挺想当兵，一是到了部队可以发衣服，二是可以不去农村插队。十六岁的我，一米七〇的个头，体检不仅合格，而且还是特别棒，因此把我分到了西藏阿里地区，就是孔繁森后来工作过的地方。

穿上绿军装的那天，我们这些新兵就踏上了西行的路。满以为乘军列可以直达新疆乌鲁木齐，没想到军列竟站站停车让行，好不容易才到了目的地，一部分女兵留在这里，另一部分要翻过天山到南疆喀什。这段路程更难走，没有了火车，要坐六天汽车，我又晕车，那种难受的劲头，不堪回首。到了喀什进行短暂的新兵训练后，只挑五个女兵去阿里当卫生兵，许多人表决心，写决心书，争着抢着要当卫生兵。我没有表态，倒不是害怕去阿里，而是不想当卫生兵，我觉得整天和愁眉苦脸的病人打交道，不如当通信兵爬电线杆自在。万万没想到这次却挑到我头上了。那时我们没有选择的自由，只有服从安排。

我前面讲羡慕你们，还包括羡慕你们今天有许多选择的机会，未来的命运是掌握在你们自己的手里。你们喜欢做什么，是科学家，还是工程师，你们只要好学上进，脚踏实地去努力，就一定能够实现自己的愿望。要知道，一个人一生能从事自己所爱好的又对人类有用的职业，是非常幸福的事。不过，无论是现在还是将来，人的一生总会遇到不遂个人心意的安排，那么你该怎么办？当时，我是一方面服从安排，努力做好卫生兵的工作；另一方面没有放弃个人的目标与爱好，并为将来有机会实现个人目标创造条件。后来，我被任命为卫生兵班的班长，又踏上了去阿里的山路。

阿里，平均海拔五千米以上，是地球上海拔最高的地区，面积有三十五万平方千米，相当于江苏省面积的三点二倍，而人口却只有三万人，是中国最地广人稀的地方。从北京这个文明繁华的都市，一下子来到中国最荒凉、最偏远、杳无人烟的地方生活，反差太大了。在这里放眼望去是无穷无尽的高山，千年不化的寒冰，然而却难以见到生命的痕迹。在这里生活是极其艰难的，一年四季，穿着一身无法更换的棉衣。在这里行军拉练，一天竟要走一百二十千米路。这在平原走起来，都吃不消，而在高原缺氧的情况下，还要负重，扛着枪、卫生箱、饭锅、米袋和棉靴，这对一个女兵来说，又是何等艰苦。在那种恶劣的环境下，又在超越了生命承受的极限时，我甚至有过死的念头。行军休息，一坐下去就再也不想起来了，可是那寒冷的地方，行军时可以穿单鞋，休息时立即要换上棉靴，否则脚就会被冻坏。这里终年难以吃上一口青菜，更没有零食，仅有的脱水菜，一旦泡出来就成了烂泥，难以下咽。许多战友将年轻的生命永远地留在了那冰川雾岭之间。

我当卫生员，为了掌握医学知识，就要学人体解剖学。我们是在医生的带领下，抬着尸体爬到高山顶上，才有机会认识人的机体内各种器官、神经、血管的部位与特征，这是在战胜险恶、恐惧后，才获得与积累了的医疗经验。

在这片广袤无垠的高原上，十一年艰苦生活的锻炼，是无数人的奉献与牺牲，才使我们懂得做人的责任，领悟到真理与庄严、崇高与伟大、勇敢与坚强的内涵。人生可能有许多事情还难以选择和把握，但有一点，人是可以选择和把握的，那就是自己对人生的态度。只有积极地、向上地、友善地、努力地、乐观地、充满信心地去对待生活，人生才会有亮色，这也是我这段西部生活的价值。

女学生：

请给我们介绍一下您的第一部作品《昆仑殇》的创作过程，以及您的处女作是怎样出版的。

毕淑敏：

一九八〇年，我从西藏阿里转业回北京。此前，我在部队的医学院校进行过系统的专业学习，成了一名医生，因此回京后，我被分在一家工厂的卫生所做内科主治医生，后来又当上了卫生所所长。回京也好，当医生、所长也好，我魂牵梦萦的仍然是西藏阿里的那段生活，它留在我生命中的痕迹太深刻了，我非常想把那里的故事告诉别人，我想把它写出来。

人做任何事情前，当然应冷静地想想自己的底儿怎样。我当医生很自信，是个态度与医术都不错的医生。可是要写书了，心中就没有了底。因为我没读过大学中文课，写作的底子又薄，于是我决定在从医的同时，自学电大中文系的课程。电视大学的教学方式很好，采取一种开放的、灵活的教授形式，我只用了一年半的时间就把原来需要三年学完的课程全部读完了，而且成绩还很好。

那时，我一个学期主修了九门课，老师感到惊奇。因为脱产的学生一学期一般也就能学完五门课。由于我的学习态度好，不是为文凭，而是为了积累自己的本事，为了把那些刻骨铭心的阿里生活早些写出来告诉世人，所以在学习上不敢有丝毫懈怠，有些知识老师说不重要（对考试而言），我仍然认真对待它们。

一九八六年，在我三十四岁时，我开始了小说《昆仑殇》的写作。我把这部小说的结构、语言、情节、故事、人物、对话等等小说必备的要素，都想得比较清楚，然后再把它们组合起来。由于写的是我的生活的真实经历与感受，所以写得很顺利、流畅，一气呵成。

小说写成后，面临一个大问题就是向哪家出版社投稿。我的朋友、亲戚都来帮我出主意。当时，大家有一种担心，怕和出版社没有关系，出版社不理睬我的稿件，就纷纷帮我找关系。而我这时反而十分冷静，我决定什么后门也不找，我就是要拿着自己的稿件，请素昧平生的编辑部的人来鉴定我的作品。我写这部小说，是因为我热爱曾经有过的生活，热爱写作，没有任何功利思想，是受一颗圣洁的心灵的驱动。如果在我热爱的事业中，掺进我不喜欢的举动，这就是对我圣洁心灵的亵渎，我不能这样做。于是，我把稿子投寄到解放军文艺出版社的一份刊物——《昆仑》杂志，这是全军唯一的大型文艺刊物。

稿子寄出后，大概是第三天，我得到出版社的回信，上面写着："毕淑敏同志，来稿收到，当日读完，被本文庞大的气势和沉重的主题所震撼，请速来编辑部。"并要求我携同丈夫一起去编辑部面谈稿件修改事宜。这使我大感不解，为什么这事还要丈夫保驾。后来，解放军文艺出版社的社长告诉我，他们当时看到这篇小说后，觉得写这篇作品的作者至少有十年以上的创作经验，他们不相信作者是一位初学写作的人；另外，文中写到的那种艰苦卓绝的军旅生活，不可能出自一位女作者之手，怀疑是我的丈夫替我写的。在编辑部交谈的过程中，每个细节，我都侃侃而谈，而我的先生则在一旁进入了半睡眠状态，他们相信了作者真的是我。这就是最初写作与出版的过程。

顺便提一句，从那时起至后来十余年写作的时间里，我写了不少小说与散文，大约两百万字。其间，我觉得自己的文学功底还需加厚，就又去考研，攻读了文学硕士学位。

女学生：

您的作品写了许多震撼人心的人物，他们在现实中是否都有生活原型？一个作家怎样才能写出对公众有益的好作品？

毕淑敏：

我的作品如果是散文，基本都是真实的，因为散文往往是人的真情的表达，它以真实为前提，真实是散文的一种品格。而小说体裁，会有一些虚构的人物、场景、情节、故事等。无论是散文还是小说，都是心灵深处有感而发的。从这个意义上讲，作者在散文、小说中表达出来的情感都是真实的。

谈到如何把作品写好，我赞同一位老作家的意见，作家应该把对于人的关怀和热情、悲悯化为冷静的处理。作家不是牢骚满腹、呻吟颤抖、刺头反骨、躁狂的"伟人"。我借用这话来说明作家的社会责任，或者讲作者写作应有的态度，没有这种责任和态度是难以写好作品的。

记得有这样一句话，"世界上并不缺少美，而是缺少发现"。这话听起来好像很抽象，其实在生活中，我们对周围发生的事，虽有多种多样的看法，但更重要的是能发现一些新见解、新认识。作为作者或作家，一定要在自己的文章中表达和凸显自己独特的认识。一个作品最忌讳没有新意，只是重复别人的陈词。

比如，人对死亡的恐惧是一种普遍心理，我作为一名医生，行医二十多年，看到人在生命的晚期，那种苍凉、恐惧的表现，对活着的人和即将离去的人心理压力都是极大的，因此，我写了《预约死亡》这篇小说。我把死亡看成人成长的最后阶段，死亡不是不可思议的，而是很正常的生命现象。对于死亡，人们应有一种冷静、镇静的态度，从而有尊严地度过一生，有尊严地走过人生的最后阶段。这是我的见解，这是我作为作家要用笔传达的对死亡的关怀，对人健康心理的关注。

女学生：

假如您的作品没有被出版社选中，假如您的文章没有被读者认同，您会如何对待？

毕淑敏：

这个问题我已经被人问过很多次，我觉得要试着去干一件事，总会有两种可能，一种是完全没有经验，就试着干，叫摸着石头过河，一次不成功，我再做，两次不成功，我还做，一直干下去。我好像不是这种类型的人，我喜欢在我已知的情况下，或者说是做好所有的准备工作的前提下，才开始去干。就像跳高一样，有的人跳一米的高度，跳了很多次都跳不过去，也许在跳过二十次后，才跳过去。而我首先会在跳高前揣摩优秀跳高运动员的跳跃姿势，然后会去模仿，再试着做一下助跑，领会要领之后，我再去跳。第一次跳，我起码要有百分之五十的把握，如果是完全没有把握的事，我不会去做。

我学习写作时已三十四岁了，如果再年轻一些，可以更激进些，初生牛犊不怕虎嘛。由于年龄所限，我就要做更完善、全面的准备，因此写作前我读电大，写作中又读文学硕士学位，这都是在做起跳的准备。

毕淑敏 13

有人还问过我，如果当时你一投不中、二投不中、三投不中，你会怎么办？我估计三投不中，我就不干了，因为我已尽了所有的努力。比如一投不中，我会想是不是编辑眼光不行，我可能要找其他编辑部；如果大家都看不中，说明我不是写作的材料，我会急流勇退的。

一次，一位外国学者问我，你是否想过要获得诺贝尔奖。我直截了当地告诉他，没有想过。这位学者很奇怪，他说，不想获大奖，你如何去努力呢？我的回答是，这好比我们这些人，谁都不可能打破刘易斯、约翰逊的百米世界纪录，但这并不影响我们每个人竭尽全力去跑出百米的最好成绩。因为我们每个人都要珍惜生命，珍惜上天给我们的这份经历，珍爱自己的爱好，全力以赴，努力达到我们可能达到的最好成绩，这就是人的生命意义之所在。而不一定要以外在的某种框架和他人的评价，作为自己是否成功的标准。我们不仅要注重收获，更要注重耕耘。

Keep Looking on the Bright Side

Bi Shumin:

This is the first time I am meeting with girls from high school. I am very excited. Now, before you start shooting questions at me, let me say a few words.

First of all, let me say that I envy you your age. You would say: "What is there to envy? Actually we envy you! You are independent, you don't have to listen to your parents ... "

I really mean it when I say that I envy you. When young, one is full of vitality, lapping up knowledge, living through the perfect period for growth in intelligence — advantages that are not available at the touch of a button anytime, anywhere, and this precious period is so fleeting!

In a word, I want you to appreciate your time in high school.

Another remark I wish to make is that, generally speaking, girls are more sensitive than boys. The girl appreciates the world with her whole heart — the success and the failure, the happiness and the sorrow, and she lets them penetrate her very soul. This psychological aspect of the female gender leads them to see the world or take action in terms of emotion or instinct. But the world is not an everlasting spring. Sometimes the days are cold and the sky is clouded. Problems appear and block your path and girls are more susceptible. Therefore, girls must have determination and will power if they want to grasp the bright side of life and have a career.

Girl student:

Thank you for your words of advice coming from the heart. We have great respect for you, we love your books and we envy you for your rich experience of life. My question is, how did you spend your high school years, and how did it affect your present success?

Bi Shumin:

I attended the high school attached to the Beijing Foreign Language Institute. It used to be situated within the precincts of what used to be the Hepingmen High School thirty years ago. At the time, it was fashionable to study a foreign language, and even to concentrate on one foreign language as a major, though the competition was keen. As for the high school attached to the Institute, there was one spot to be contested among four hundred students, and I was the lucky one to be accepted. The school was strange in one way — the proportion of male students took up more than 70% of the student body. As far as I can remember, there were only nine girls in my class.

At the time, the concept of "lady first" was unknown among the male population. Girls had to be exceptional or they would be totally ignored. It is a sign of inequality between the sexes. The situation nowadays is of course much improved, but even so, there is no heaven sent new world of perfect equality between men and women. If women want a place in the world, they must rely on their own efforts to achieve it.

When I was pursuing my studies at the junior high level, the school suddenly stopped operations. I had always loved studies since childhood, and my grades had been satisfactory. What I feared was exams, especially exams by foreign teachers, who were unpredictable in the tests that they conduct so that no matter how well you are prepared, the tests always took us by surprise. But on this occasion, as we were preparing for exams, suddenly it was announced that there would be no exams. How we rejoiced! But later as the days dragged on and we just spent time in chitchat, we got sick and tired of the idle days.

There was a good library in our school. According to

library rules, whenever you take out a book, you must include a short summary of the contents when you return it. If you do not fulfil this request, you will not be allowed to continue borrowing from the library. However, this request did not stop us from borrowing. A group of us girls would go to the library and each of us would bring back a book and pass it around.

Acting against my conscience, I came up with rigmarole to meet the demands of the library. I remember that once in order to qualify for continuous borrowing, I borrowed a copy of "War and Peace" and wrote a piece saying that Tolstoy was floating the idea of "bourgeois humanism" and that his erroneous ideas appeared glaringly on page 50, of which I offer an example as follows, and I would quote one of Tolstoy's sayings. Then I would go on to page 145 and quote another of Tolstoy's sayings. Because I had read the books very carefully and even took down some notes, to this day I can remember some passages. Thus I secured the trust of the librarian and borrowed more books, following a cycle of borrowing, reading, and returning the books. My classmates got tired of writing down reading notes to secure the books, and over time gave up going to the Library. But they still wanted to read the books, and one day a classmate came up with an idea: "Let's have Bi Shumin tell us a story every night from the stories that she has read."

Thus I started to tell a story lasting one hour every evening and kept up the practice, like those instalments on radio.

I had narrated the story of "The Man who Laughs," One of my classmates, now in the US, told me that once she had heard me tell that story, she did not want to read the book anymore, my recital being so vivid. Thinking back, I realize how I myself had benefitted from that practice, because since I had to tell and retell the story, I read with great care and made sure that I could transmit the story in every detail. Those three years when school was cut off, I read many great classics of literature, recited many of the stories to my classmates, improved my skill at language, laid the basis for a writing career and brushed up my oratory skills as well. The classics are the records of the wisdom of our ancestors, their perception of life, their knowledge of the world ... taken down in writing. It is like fire, lighting up our way through life, an inspiration to those who follow, handed down generation after generation. It is the fire illuminating human civilization as it seeks for self-perfection.

Girl student:

It is said that you had been a soldier and had also served as a military medic. What is the merit of a life like that?

Bi Shumin:

I was born in a military family. One might say

that my education and my character are owing to my parents. It was life on the highlands of Ngari in the west which had formed my character.

It was winter of 1968 when the conscription was launched. I was very keen to join the army, the reason being that I would get free uniforms in the army and I would escape being sent down as an "educated youth." I was sixteen at the time, 1.7 meters tall and very healthy, so I was dispatched to the Ngari area in Tibet.

We headed west after we got into our uniforms, expecting to be taken to Urumqi by car. But the car kept stopping to give way to traffic and we had a long trip. When we arrived at what I thought was our destination, some of us girl soldiers stopped and was stationed here while the rest of us had to cross a mountain and make our way to Kashgar in south Xinjiang. That segment of our trip was very hard, six days by car, and I was carsick. That painful journey! The memory was unbearable. Arriving at Kashgar, we got some brief training and five girls among us would be ordered to work in Ngari as military medics. Many of the girls among us volunteered for the job but I did not volunteer. Not that I disliked Ngari, but I did not want to be a military medic. Rather than be stuck with sickly people, I would rather be in communications and climb telephone poles. Unfortunately, I was picked to be a military medic and I had no choice but to obey orders.

I had mentioned earlier that I envy you people; actually I envy you for having more choices. Your future is in your own hands. So long as you study hard, you can be whatever you want to be: scientist, engineer … So long as you work hard, you will reach your goal. You must know that if a person could pursue a career of his or her own choice and still serve the society, he or she is a lucky person. However, whether or in the future, one is bound to come up against unwelcome things. What should one do? In my own case, I obeyed orders and worked as a military medic, but still kept up my own interest, so as to be prepared once the chance turns up. Later I was assigned to be the head of the nurses group. We continued our way up Ngari mountain.

Ngari prefecture has an average elevation of five thousand meters above sea level, the highest on earth, covering 350 thousand square kiometres, 3.5 times the area of Jiangsu province, but the population only thirty thousand — the most thinly populated place in China.

Coming from Beijing, the capital, and arriving at the most remote, thinly populated spot in the country, was a great shock. All one could see were mountains and unmelted snow, with few signs of life. Life was hard. Throughout the four seasons, dressed in the same cotton-padded jacket, we underwent training, sometimes covering one hundred and twenty kilometres a day. It would be a trial even on the plains, not to mention going through training on the heights where you were required to carry your gun, your medical container, your food container, your cooking pot, your rice bag and your cotton-padded shoes. What a trial it had been for the girl-soldiers in training — beyond human endurance. Sometimes I had been pushed beyond the edge and had wanted to end it all. When there was a break during the march, we would be unwilling to get up. Surprisingly, under the freezing temperature, we walked in thin walking shoes but had to change into cotton-padded shoes the minute we stopped for a break, or else our feet would be frostbitten. All year round, it was hard to get a bit of fresh veggies, not to mention any snacks. It was frozen vegetables only, which turned into a soggy mess when lifted out of the water, and was totally inedible. Many of my comrades had laid down their young lives forever among the frozen rivers and the foggy mountains of Tibet.

I had to learn basic human anatomy as part of my medical training to become an army medic. I did it the hard way, under treacherous conditions and overcoming fears. For an opportunity to study the locations and characteristics of various body organs, nerves, and blood vessels, we had to carry a cadaver all the way up to a mountaintop spot, led by an army doctor.

Eleven years of harsh life on the vast, boundless plateau, and the dedication and sacrifice of many others, gave me a keen sense of duty as a human being, and a deep appreciation of truth, dignity, magnanimity, valour and fortitude. There are many things in life that are beyond our control and not of our choosing. But we can certainly choose and decide our attitude towards life. Only by adopting a positive, upbeat, kind-hearted, proactive, optimistic and confident attitude will we see more bright side of life. Such is the value of my stint of living in the far west of China.

Girl student:

Can you tell us a bit about the writing process of your debut novella *Mourning on Mount Kunlun* and how you got it published?

Bi Shumin:

I returned to Beijing in 1980 after my military discharge in Ngari, Tibet. Since I had been a doctor, having received a systematic training in the army medical college, I landed a job as the attending physician in a factory clinic and later became its director. Yet, my years of life in Ngari, Tibet were on my mind all the time, even though I had settled into life in Beijing, working as a physician and then clinic head. They were deeply etched in my memory. I was dying to tell the story of my life there and put it all in writing.

Before embarking on anything new, everyone should assess cool-headedly if he has it in him to succeed. I had a lot of confidence in my self as a doctor, competent and with a good attitude. To embark on literary writing, I wasn't so certain. I had never studied Chinese at the college level and did not have strong writing skills. So I decided to enrol in a program offered by the Chinese Department of the Open University, while continuing my day job in medicine. The program was open and flexible in its teaching arrangement and it took me only one and a half years to complete the program with good grades that would otherwise require three years.

I managed to complete nine courses within one semester, which surprised my instructors. Even fulltime students usually could manage only five courses in one semester. I worked hard, with a goal of preparing myself to write and share with the world the story of my life in Ngari, not merely for getting a diploma. I spared no efforts, even on topics that were less important (to succeeding in exams, that is) according to the instructors.

I began writing *Mourning on Mount Kunlun* in 1986, the year I turned thirty-four. I had thought through all the elements of the story — its structure, language, plot, storyline, characters and dialogues, before putting all the pieces together. The writing itself was smooth and unhindered, with an uninterrupted flow, for it was a story of my real life experience and feelings.

After I put down the last word, the biggest question became where I should send the manuscript. My friends and family relations all had their two pennies. They worried that I wouldn't get a response from any publisher since I did not have connections. There was collective head-scratching for possible contacts. I was rather calm myself and decided against any backdoor dealing. I would simply submit my manuscript to editors I had never met before for their evaluation. What motivated me to write the novella were my love for the life I had led and a passion for writing. I was driven by a pure soul. I had no yearning for fame and fortune. I wouldn't let anything I detested to taint my literary endeavour, which would have amounted to blasphemy. There was no way I would allow that to happen. So I sent my manuscript through the mail to the *Kunlun* Magazine that belonged to the Literature and Art Publishing House of the People's Liberation Army, the only major literary journal published by the armed forces.

Three days later, I received a reply that read, "Dear Comrade Bi Shumin, Thank you for your manuscript. We read through the novella on the day of receipt and were touched by the broad sweep of the storyline and its sombre subject matter. Please come to the editorial department for a chat at your earliest."

I was invited for a discussion on some rewrites, to be accompanied by my husband. I was puzzled by the hubby part of the invitation and wondered why that was necessary. It turned out that they suspected my husband had been the ghost writer, assuming that such a story of the extremely harsh military life could only be written by someone with at least ten years of writing experience, and not by some novice or a female writer, so the head of the publishing house later told me. However, they were eventually convinced of my authorship, for throughout the discussion, I was able to elaborate with ease on all the details of the story, while my husband, sitting next to me, wandered into the region of half sleep. That's the long and short of it.

I have since written quite a number of novels, short stories and essays, totalling two million Chinese ideograms, over the period of more than a decade. In the meantime, believing my literary skills can do with some improvement, I enrolled in a post graduate program and earned my master of art in literature.

Girl student:

There are many deeply moving characters in your stories. Were they all real life personalities? How can a writer create great stories that benefit the public?

Bi Shumin:

My essays, being reflections of true feelings,

are mostly factual and true. Truthfulness is a prerequisite and an inherent quality of good essay writing. Novels inevitably have fictional characters, scenarios, plots and storylines. However, an author's writing, be it in essay or novel form, should be driven by genuine feelings from deep within. In such sense, what is rendered in essays and novels should both be genuine, too.

As for how one can produce good writings, I agree with what a veteran writer once suggested: a writer should turn his concern, passion and sympathy for fellow humans into calm musings and elaboration. A literary writer is not a superhuman with license to whine and be grumpy, rebellious, seditious, and fervent. I borrow his words to highlight an author's social responsibility, or rightful attitude, barring which he cannot expect to create good writings.

I remember the quote on beauty. "Beauty is everywhere. It is not that she is lacking to our eye, but our eyes fail to perceive her." This may sound rather abstract. In fact, it points to the importance of originality; the ability to elicit the new and true in the myriad phenomena and views that surround us. An author must try to express something that is unique. The greatest taboo in literary writing is the lack of originality — repeating what has been said before.

I have written about death, which invariably incites fear. Having worked in medicine for more than two decades, I had seen the emptiness and fear that people experienced in the last stage of their life, which put tremendous psychological pressure on both the living and departing. Therefore, I wrote the novella *An Appointment with Death*, in which death is treated as a natural phenomenon and the final phase of life, not something unthinkable. We should adopt a calm, assured attitude towards death and live and go through the final stage of life with dignity. This is my point of view, and my concern for death and psychological wellbeing that I, as a writer, wish to convey through writing.

Girl student:

What if your manuscript had been rejected by the publishing house or your writings had not been well received by readers?

Bi Shumin:

I have been asked this question many times before. I believe there are generally two approaches to any new venture. The first is that, without any prior experience, you start by trial and error, trying to cross the river by feeling the stones and not giving up, despite repeated setbacks, before eventual success. This is not my type. The second is to make all the necessary preparations before you plunge in, which I prefer. For example, to attempt a high jump of, say, one meter, I would first study the approach and take-off of excellent high jumpers, emulate their techniques, try them out and attempt a jump only after I have understood all the techniques, unlike those who keep attempting their jumps until they clear the height after failing perhaps two dozen times. I will not attempt my jump unless I know I have a half and half chance for success. I will not attempt anything if I have zero self-assurance of success.

I was thirty-four when I embarked on creative writing. Had I been a little younger, I might have been more adventurous, like an oblivious and fearless buffalo calf. Because of my age, I needed to get better and more thoroughly prepared. Therefore I took an undergraduate course with the Open University and acquired a master of art in literature while writing fulltime, which all amounted to preparations before the high jump takeoff.

Someone once asked me what I would have done if my manuscript had been rejected repeatedly. I guess I would have thrown in the towel after my manuscript was rejected for the third time. At the first rejection, I would have doubted the editor's judgement and continued trying other publishers. If I got rejections from them all, it would have shown I was no wordsmith material. I would have quitted before too late.

A foreign scholar once asked me if I ever wanted to win the Nobel Prize. I replied flatly, "No, it has never occurred to me." He was quite surprised, saying, "How do you keep up your endeavour if you don't want to win the big prize?" I said to him, "None of us, for example, can break the records for the 100-meter sprint set by Ben Johnson or Carl Lewis, but that won't stop us from going all out for our personal best in 100-meter sprint."

We should all cherish life, cherish the past that we are blessed with, cherish and be dedicated to our individual pursuits so that we may all achieve the best that we are capable of. This is our mark of success and where the meaning of life lies, which shouldn't be subject to any external frame of reference or judgement by others. In the end, the journey and doing is more important than the outcome.

莺鸟与铁星

在南太平洋的岛屿中，飞翔着一种有着动听鸣叫声的美丽小鸟，叫作莺鸟，它们长着形色各异的喙。岛屿上物产丰富的日子，莺鸟们靠吃多种草籽为生，活得优哉游哉。

但是，饥馑来了。干旱袭击了岛屿，整个大地好像是刚刚凝固的炽热火山，赤红的土地，看不到一丝绿色。

科学家找到一些从前研究过的莺鸟，它们的腿上拴着铁环。观测结果，发现莺鸟们的体重大减，挣扎在死亡线上。原因是食物奇缺，能吃的都吃光了，唯一剩下的是一种叫作蒺藜的草籽。它浑身是锋利的硬刺，锐不可当。在深深的内核里隐藏的种仁，好像美味的巧克力封死在铁匣中。

蒺藜还有一个名字叫作"铁星"，象征着难以攻克。拉丁文的意思是"挤压和疼痛"。

莺鸟用自己柔弱的喙，啄开一粒铁星，先要把它顶在地上，又咬又扭，然后顶住岩石，上喙发力，下喙挤压，直到精疲力竭才能把外壳拧掉，吃到活命的粮草。

岛上开始了残酷的生存之战。没有刀光剑影，唯一的声音就是嗑碎蒺藜的噼啪声。很多莺鸟饿死了，有些顽强地生存下来。科学家想，生和死的区别在哪里呢？

经过详尽研究，喙长十一毫米的莺鸟，就能够嗑开铁星，而喙长十点五毫米的莺鸟，就望"星"兴叹，无论如何都叩不开生命森严的大门。

零点五毫米之差，就决定了莺鸟的生死存亡。在丰衣足食的时候，一切都被温柔地遮盖了，但月亮并不总是圆的，事物的规律跌宕起伏。

我猜想，那些饿死的莺鸟在最后时分，倘能思索，一定万分后悔自己为什么没能生就一个长长的利喙！短喙的莺鸟，是天生的，它们遭到了大自然无情的淘汰。但人类的喙——我们思维的强度，历练的经验，广博的智慧，强健的体力，合作的风采，幽默的神韵……却是可以在日复一日的积累中，渐渐地磨炼增长，成为我们度过困厄的支柱。

Finches and Tack-weed Seed

A species of the finches, outstanding songsters with bills of varying depth and colour, are found on an archipelago in the Pacific. Generally sedate foragers, they feed mostly on plant seeds, when the climate is conducive to lush vegetation.

Then the islands were hit by a severe and prolonged drought and the land was scorched, with not a patch of green left. It was a harsh time for the tiny songbirds.

Scientists found some of the birds that they had marked with metal rings to their legs in previous field research. They noted significant weight loss in the starving birds. The seeds they used to feed on had all but disappeared, except those of the tack-weed, which were encased in nutlets with sharp spines, as delectable chocolates secured in tin boxes. Also called caltrop, its Latin name tribulus originally meant a spiky weapon.

It would take tremendous efforts from the finches to break open the hard shells of caltrop seeds. They would press a shell against the rock or pebble for leverage and extract the seeds by tweaking and prizing with their beaks. It was all very exhausting for the birds.

The sound of caltrop nutlets cracking must have marked the battle for survival. The drought killed most of the finches, but the tougher ones survived on caltrop seeds. Scientists wanted to find out what made a difference between survival and death in the drought year.

After exhaustive research, they noted that finches with beaks of at least 11 mm in length can break open a caltrop while those with beaks of 10.5

mm weren't seen trying to eat caltrop seeds, eventually being barred from having any chance for survival.

The difference of a mere 0.5 mm in beak depth saved some finches from death. In times of plenty, such a difference meant nothing. However, natural conditions change, as certain as the waxing and waning of the moon.

I like to think that the finches in their dying moments must have regretted not having longer beaks, should they have the power of thought. The finches with shallow beaks, also the result of natural selection, ended up suffering greater selective mortality. As humans, we can consciously train ourselves; acquiring experience, physical power, mental fortitude, wisdom, collaborative mindset and humour, which will tide us over in times of extreme hardship.

节气是一种命令

夏初，买菜。老人对我说，买我的吧。看他的菜摊，好似堆积着银粉色的乒乓球，西红柿摞成金字塔样。拿起一个，柿蒂部羽毛状的绿色，很翠硬地硌着我的手。我说，这么小啊，还青，远没有冬天时我吃的西红柿好呢。

老人显著地不悦了，说，冬天的西红柿算什么西红柿呢？吃它们哪里是吃菜？分明是吃药啊。我很惊奇，说，怎么是药呢？它们又大又红，灯笼一般美丽啊。老人说，那是温室里煨出来的，先用炉火烤，再用药熏。让它们变得不合规矩地胖大，用保青剂或是保红剂，让它比画的还好看。人里面有汉奸，西红柿里头也有奸细呢。冬天的西红柿就是这种假货。

我惭愧了，多年以来，被蔬菜中的骗局所蒙蔽。那吃什么菜好呢？我虚心讨教。老人的生意很清淡，乐得教诲我，口中吐钉一般说道——记着，永远吃正当节令的菜。萝卜下来就吃萝卜，白菜下来就吃白菜。节令节令，节气就是令啊！夏至那天，太阳一定最长。冬至那天，亮光一定最短。你能不信吗？不信不行。你是冬眠的狗熊，到了惊蛰，一定会醒来。你是一条长虫，冷了就得冻僵，会变得像拐棍一样打不了弯。人不能心贪，你用了种种的计策，在冬天里，抢先吃了只有夏天才长的菜；夏天到了，怎么办呢？再吃冬天的菜吗？颠了个儿，你费尽心机，不是整个瞎忙活吗？别心急，慢慢等着吧，一年四季的菜，你都能吃到。更不要说，只有野地里，叫风吹绿的菜叶，太阳晒红的果子，才是最有味道的。

我买了老人家的西红柿，慢慢地向家中走。他的西红柿虽是露地长的，质量还有推敲的必要，但他的话浸着一种晚风的霜凉，久久伴着我。阳光斜照在网兜上，那略带柔软的银粉色，被勒割出精致的纹路，好像一幅生长的印谱。

人生也是有节气的啊。

春天就做春天的事情，去播种。秋天就做秋天的事情，去收获。快乐的时候笑，悲伤的时分洒泪。

少年需率真，过于老成，好比施用了植物催熟剂，早早定了型，抢先上市，或许能卖个好价钱，但植株不会高大，叶片不会密匝，从根本上说，该归入早夭的一列。老年太轻狂，好似理智的幼稚症。让人疑心脑内的某一部分让岁月的虫蛀了，连缀不起精彩的长卷，包裹不住漫长的人生。

世俗有句话——您看起来比实际的岁数年轻，听的人把它当作一句恭维或是赞美的话，说的人把它当作万灵的廉价礼物。我总猜这句话的背后，缩着一张上帝的笑脸。比实际的年龄年轻，就分明是好的、美的、值得庆贺的吗？小的人希冀长大，老的人祈望年轻。这种希望变更的子午线，究竟坐落在哪一扇生日的年轮？与其费尽心机地寻找秘诀，不如退而结网，锻造出心灵与年龄的同步舞蹈。

老是走向死亡的阶梯，但年轻也是临终一跃长长的助跑。五十步笑百步，不必有过多的惆怅或是优越。年轻年老都是生命的流程，不必厚此薄彼，显出对某道工序的青睐或是鄙弃，那是对造物者的大不敬，是一种浅薄而又愚蠢的势利。人们可以濡养肌体

45

的青春，但不要忘记心灵的疲倦。

死亡是生命的最后过程，有如银粉色的西红柿被摘下以后，在夕阳中渐渐地蔓延成浓烈的红色，此刻只有相信，坚定不移地服从节气的指挥。

Rhythm of Seasons

An old man, a vendor peddling his produce in the street early in the summer, called out to me, "Buy mine." He had tomatoes piled neatly in a pyramid in front of him. All ping-pong sized, they looked unripe with a silvery green sheen. I picked up one; its green sepals covered in short hairs prickly to my fingers. "They are so small," said I. "And they are green; nowhere near the ripe tomatoes I had in winter."

The old man was not impressed, "The winter ones are no comparison. They aren't even good for eating. You might as well take chemical pills!"

"What do you mean by chemical pills?" I was startled.

"They were large, bright red, as the red lanterns."

"They were all grown in heated greenhouses till they reach their unusually large sizes. Then they were gassed with ethylene that made them turn red; pretty as painted. As there are ruffians among people, they are the bad tomatoes."

Humbled, I realized I had been scammed for years by this veggie conspiracy. "Are there any vegetables good to eat at all?" asked I meekly. His business being slow, the old man was more than willing to part with a bit of free advice. "Remember," he went on like a Dutch uncle, "eat only what is in season; white radish, Napa cabbage and what not, but only when they are in season. There is a time for everything. The summer solstice is the day with the longest sunlight and the winter solstice the shortest. You have to follow the dictates of nature. Bears wake up from winter sleep when snow starts to melt. A snake that has no way of keeping warm goes into its den when it is cold. You shouldn't be greedy, wanting summer vegetables in winter. What do you do when summer comes? Eat winter vegetables? You turn things upside down to no purpose. If you have patience, you will have vegetables in all seasons. Besides, vegetables that ripen naturally in the sun and warm air always taste best."

I bought some of his tomatoes and walked home in no haste. Even though they were all grown outdoors, their quality left a lot to be desired. The old man's words lingered in the cool breeze. In the slanting sunlight, the silvery green tomatoes in the net bag took on the pattern of its knitted lines like some intricate engraving.

Life also has its seasonal rhythms. You plough and sow in the spring and harvest in the fall. You laugh in jubilation and weep in sorrow.

When you are young, if you act reserved and with a sophisticated air, rather than innocence and candour, you are no different from vegetables artificially made to ripen. They may fetch a good price for getting to the market earlier. Yet being premature, they will not be naturally flavourful, doomed to perish early, too. Likewise, when a man who has got some years behind him acts senselessly and whimsically, you will likely suspect he is a bit off his head. The tapestry of his life is threadbare and tattered and will not last till the end.

You often hear people describe someone looking younger than his or her age; flattering words easily dispensed and welcomed. However, I have always thought that when such platitudes were uttered, God must have laughed. Is looking younger than one's age always good, beautiful and worth celebrating? The young wish to grow old, the old young. Where does the meridian of such diverging aspirations lie? Maybe the question itself is moot. We should perhaps all think and act our age.

If aging is the last flight of ascending stairs to death, then youth is but the long ramp before the final ascent. Whether old or young, no one should feel and act superior to another, like the pot calling the kettle black, when it comes to age. You may keep your skin and body looking young, but don't forget your soul can be weary. Aging is a natural process of life; you do not exult one phase and denigrate another. It would be too shallow, foolish and mean; the ultimate of irreverence for the Creator.

Death is the final phase of life, like the silvery green tomatoes turning a rich, brilliant red after harvest in the setting sun. At such moments, your thoughts invariably dwell on the dictates of nature, the rhythm of the seasons.

梳理生命之序

曾听到一位患过"非典"的香港心脏科医生谈起他的感受。因为病情突变，他住进了医院的"深切治疗部"。"深切治疗"这个词，内地很少用，估计那意思是病情笃重，需要更深入的治疗和更关切的照料。词是温煦的，但缝隙间掩藏着的凶氛，还是幽幽地散了出来。

医生脱险后接受采访，记者问，一个人孤独地住在病房里，想了些什么？医生沉吟了一会儿说，想得最多的是，要把人生中最重要的事和一般的事分开，先做那些重要的事情。记者当然追问，你生命中最重要的事是什么呢？医生答，和我的家人在一起。

我听了以后，愣了很久。医生传达和重复了一个直白到简陋的真理——事情是可以排顺序的。生死边缘，回眸一望，常常发现玉石俱焚，鱼龙混杂，重要的事被疏漏了，不重要的事却被无限放大。

几天后，我又见到一位脚夫老人。大家都熟悉的陕北民歌《赶牲灵》，就是脚夫们走沟穿壑在高原上吼出的。他说"活着做遍，死了无怨"，意思是人活着的时候，把你想做的事都做了，就一生完满，活得够本，可以安然地死了。

医生是留洋博士，脚夫满面黄尘苍凉。不同层面的人，异曲同工的话，于是在突如其来的瘟疫背后，就有了哲学的味道。

人生有涯，即使没有"非典"袭扰，生命也必有大限。活着就是一个向着死亡的存在，由于有铁闸似的死亡矗立在深邃的尽头，便使我们的生命显出异样的美丽和时不我待的紧迫。人是脆弱的，种种意外的蛰伏，使得能上天入地、能让电脑每秒钟运算若干亿次的现代人却无法估算出每人大限到来的时刻。面对永恒困境，只剩下一个可行的方法，就是把那些我们以为最重要的事抓紧做完。简而言之，你要给生命排一个序。

什么是生命中最重要的事呢？夜深人静、月朗星稀之时，每个人心平气和地想想：也许是事业有成，也许是周游世界，也许是孝顺父母，也许是舍己为人，也许是永远探索，也许是安分守己……我相信每个人都会得出自己的答案。

寻找最重要的事情，其实就是寻找生命的价值。

它是我们立下的宏愿，是你选定的主牌，有了它，一应事务的顺序就排出来了。现代人陷入日常的忙碌，无数细小而琐碎的事件，缭乱了我们的双眼，模糊了我们的视线，凝滞了我们的脚步，壅塞了我们的襟怀……

Set Your Priorities Straight

I once heard a story about a cardiologist in Hong Kong who had suffered severe acute respiratory syndrome (SARS). At one time, he was placed under intensive care after his conditions deteriorated abruptly. The Chinese term for intensive care used in Hong Kong is quite different from that on the Chinese mainland. It carries a softer tone with a hint of compassion, even though it means the care for patients in precarious, critical conditions.

In a press interview after he had recovered, he was asked, "What were your thoughts when you were alone in the hospital ward?" He paused for a moment before replying: "I thought most often that I would thenceforth give priority to the most important things in life." The journalist pursued, "What is most important for you?" "To spend time with my family," replied the doctor.

This put me in a pensive mood. The doctor told us a stark, plain truth — priorities should be set straight. Verging on the brink of death, he realized that in the humdrum of life, things that matter are often overshadowed by things that don't, and that the inessentials are too often magnified.

A few days later, I met an old porter, one of those who carried heavy loads on mountain trails, immortalized in a well-known folk song of northern Shaanxi. He told me, "Do 'em all and you die with no regrets." What he meant was that if you have done all the things you want to do in life, you are prepared to die at any time in peace. Your life is worth it.

The cardiologist is a doctor with overseas

education, and the old porter a craggy countryman with a toil-ravaged face. Despite their vastly different stations in life, their words carried the same message, of philosophical meaning after we had experienced the SARS crisis that struck out of the blue.

The only thing certain in life is that it will one day end, even absent outbreaks of epidemics such as SARS. To live is to eventually face death. Yet precisely because of the iron door of death lurking at the far end, living is urgent and life all the more precious and beautiful. Humans are fragile. As the unexpected always happens, no one is certain when his hour of departure will arrive, even though mankind is now capable of travelling in space, diving into unfathomable depths, and creating supercomputers that perform hundreds of millions of FLOPS. With finality looming, it is paramount to do the most important things first and fast. Simply put, we must set our priorities in life right.

What is most important in life? It is a question that everyone should think over, in the quiet of the night, under a moonlit sky. Is it to have a successful career, travel the world, make time for one's parents, do self-sacrificing deeds, explore the unknown or lead a quiet, self-sufficient existence? I believe everyone will come up with his or her own answers.

Determining what matters most is to define the true worth of your life.

It will be your aspiration — the key to sorting out your priorities, without which we are overwhelmed by the puniness of everyday living; our eyes bleary, our feet leaden and our mind befogged because of all the detritus of life.

带上灵魂去旅行

人的知识永远是不完备的，他无法知道一个地区或是一个时代，是否就是空间和时间的全部。在这个意义上讲，我们每个人都是井底之蛙，所不同的只是栖息的这口井的直径大小而已。每个人也都是可怜的夏虫，不可语冰，于是，我们天生需要旅行。生为夏虫是我们的宿命，但不是我们的过错。在夏虫短暂的生涯中，我们可以和命运做一个商量，尽可能地把这口井掘得口径大一些，把时间和地理的尺度拉得伸展一些。就算最终不可能看到冰，夏虫也力所能及地面对无瑕的水和渐渐刺骨的秋风，想象一下冰的透明清澈与痛彻心扉的寒冻。

　　旅行，首先是一场体能的马拉松，你需要提前做很多准备。依我片面的经验，旅行的要紧物件有三种。第一，当然是时间。人们常常以为旅行最重要的前提是钱，于是就把攒钱当成旅行的先决条件。其实，没有钱或是只有少量的钱，也可以旅行。关于这一点，只要你耐心搜集，就会找到很多省钱的秘籍。如果把一个人比作一辆车，驱动我们前行的汽油，并不是金钱，而是时间。这个道理极其简单，你的时间消耗完了，你任何事都干不成了，还奢谈什么呢？或者说，那时的旅行只有一个方向，就是地心了。

　　第二桩物件，是放下忧愁。忧愁是旅行的致命杀手，人无远虑，乃可出行。忧愁是有分量的，一两忧愁可以化作万朵秤砣，绊得你跌跌撞撞鼻青脸肿。最常见的忧愁来自这样的思维：把这笔旅游的钱省下来可以买多少斤米多少篓菜，过多长时间丰衣足食的家常日子。将满足口腹之欲的时间当作计量单位，是曾经有用现在却不必坚守的习惯。很多中国人一遇到新奇又需要破费的事儿，马上把它折算成米面开销，用粮食做万变不离其宗的度量衡。积谷防饥本是美德，可什么事都提到危及生命安全的高度来考虑，活着就成了负担。谁若一意孤行去旅行，就咒你将来基本的生存都要打折，食不果腹衣不蔽体流落街头……别怪我说得凄惶，如果你打算做一次比较破费的旅行，你一定会听到这一类的谆谆告诫。迅即把诸事折合成大米的计算公式，来自温饱没有满足的农耕时代遗留下来的精神创伤。如果你一定要把所有的钱，都攒起来用于防患于未然，这是你的自由，别人无法干涉。可你要明白，身体的生理机能满足之后，就不必一味地再纠结于脏腑。总是由着身体自言自语地说那些饥饱的事儿，你就灭掉了自己去看世界的可能性，一辈子只能在肚子画出的半径中度过。这样的人生，在温饱还没有解决的往昔，是不得已而为之，甚至可能成为能优先活下来的王牌。在今天，就有时过境迁过于迂腐之感了。

第三桩事儿，是活在身体的此时此刻。此话怎讲？当下身体不错，就可以出发，抬腿走就是，不必终日琢磨以后心力衰竭的呕血和罹患癌症的剧痛。我琢磨着自己还有能力挣出些许以后治病的费用，我相信国家的社会保障机制会越来越好。我捏捏自己的胳膊腿，觉得它们尚能禁得住摔打，目前爬高上低餐风宿露不在话下。若我以后真是得了多少万人民币也医不好的重症，从容赴死就是了，临死前想想自己身手矫健耳聪目明时，也曾有过一番随心所欲的游历，奄奄一息时的情绪，也许是自豪。

我是渐渐老迈的汽车，油料所剩已然不多。我要精打细算，小心翼翼地驱动它赶路。生命本是宇宙中的一瓣微薄的睡莲，终有偃旗息鼓闭合的那一天。在这之前，我一定要抓紧时间，去看看这四野无序的大地，去会一会英辈们残留下的伟绩和废墟。

　　终于决定迈开脚步了，很多人有个习惯，出远门之前，先拿出纸笔，把自己要带的东西都一一列出。旅游秘籍中，传授这种清单的俯拾皆是。到寒带，你要带上皮手套雪地靴；到热带，你要带上防晒霜太阳镜驱蚊油。就算是不寒不热的福地，你也要带上手电筒黄连素加上使领馆的电话号码……

　　所有这些，都十分必要。可有一样东西，无论你到哪里，都不可须臾离开。那就是——你可记得带上自己的灵魂？

　　据说古老的印第安人有个习惯，当他们的身体移动得太快的时候，会停下脚步，安营扎寨，耐心等待自己的灵魂前来追赶。有人说是三天一停，有人说是七天一停，总之，人不能一味地走下去，要驻扎在行程的空隙中，和灵魂会合。灵魂似乎是个身负重担或是手脚不利落的弱者，慢吞吞地经常掉队。你走得快了，它就跟不上趟儿。我觉得此说法最有意义的部分，是证明在旅行中，我们的身体和灵魂是不同步的，是分离分裂的。而一次绝佳的旅行，自然是身体和灵魂高度协调一致，生死相依。

　　好的旅行应该如同呼吸一样自然，旅行的本质是学习，而学习是人类的本能。身为医生，我知道人一生必得不断地学习。我不当医生了，这个习惯却如同得过天花，在心中留下斑驳的痕迹。旅行让我知道在我之前活过的那些人，他们可曾想到过什么做过什么。旅行也让我知道，在我没有降生的那些岁月，大自然盛大的恩典和严酷的惩罚。旅行中我知道了人不可以骄傲，天地何其寂寥、峰峦何其高耸、海洋何其阔大。旅行中我也知晓了死亡原不必悲伤，因为你其实并没有消失，只不过以另外的方式循环往复。

凡此种种，都不是单纯的身体移动就能够解决问题的，只能留给旅行中的灵魂来做完功课。出发时，悄声提醒，背囊里务必记得安放下你的灵魂。它轻到没有一丝分量，也不占一寸地方，但重要性远胜过GPS。饥饿时是你的面包，危机时助你涉险过关。你欢歌笑语时，它也无声扮出欢颜。你捶胸顿足时，它也滴泪悲愤……灵魂就算不能像烛火一样照耀着我们的行程，起码也要同甘共苦地跟在后面，不离不弃，不能干三天停一天地磨洋工。否则，我们就是一具飘飘荡荡的躯壳在蹒跚，敲一敲，发出空洞的回音，仿佛千年前枯萎的胡杨。

Don't Leave Your Soul behind when You Travel

Man is woefully limited in his knowledge. He knows not if his personal experience has anything to do with the universal human condition in his time. He is no different from a frog dwelling at the bottom of the well; thinking that the tiny patch of light overhead is all there is to the sky. We need to wander. Although our lives are destined to be brief, ephemeral like a firefly, we can expand our lives' dimensions by travel, striking a divine bargain with Fate. We may not all reach the outermost extremities, as the firefly never survives the autumnal chill. Yet, travel gives us a fresh perspective, the clarity of mind and the sense of catharsis at the edge of the sublime, in the face of pristine glacial ice; the purging power of Nature.

Travel is a marathon, a prolonged physical exertion, for which ample preparation is a must. Then, there are three prerequisites, according to my limited experience.

First, you need time. People often think that having enough money is most important for travel. Yet in truth, you can travel without money or with only a limited amount of it. You will find plenty of DIY guides to travel on a shoestring if you care to search. The fuel for travelling is time, like petrol for a vehicle. When your time is running short, there is little you can do, let alone travel. Eventually, if one moves at all, it is one-directional: downward, to earth, to dust.

Second, put away all the worries that stifle the nomad in you. Only the carefree ranges far. A puny worry can weigh heavy on your heart. Worry turns every pebble into a stumbling block for the wayfarer. The most common worry is cost: money spent on wandering may be better spent on bags of rice and grocery, so people think. Such a mindset — considering everything from the perspective of the stomach region, something of virtue once upon a time, is what we can do without now. Many tend to put every novel undertaking on the gastronomic scale, so to speak, calculating its cost in catties of rice and flour that could be otherwise bought. Stocking up for leaner times is a virtue. But life would be so boring if it is used to discourage every attempt at wandering. It is as though someone determined to go away would inevitably deplete his store for future and be down and out. You may think I sounded unduly alarming, but you are bound to hear such advice and warnings if you ever plan any trip that costs some money. Such a mentality is really a vestige of the agrarian society where food was always scarce and famine recurrent. If you insist on saving for rainy days, you are free to do so and no one could stop you. However, humans also aspire to things beyond a happy stomach once their physiological needs are satisfied. If you never rise above your gastronomic urge, you will miss the boat to see the world. The drive to satiate hunger was crucial to survival in times of scarcity. As times have changed, such a preoccupation is passé.

Third, live in the present and do what befits your physical condition. If you are in good health, embark on your journey now. Stop worrying about the days when you will be too old and worn, about the excruciating pain of cancer. As for myself, I believe in my ability to still earn and save some money for medical needs in old age and in the nation's social security system getting better and better. I pinch my arms and legs, finding them still sturdy enough for me to set off into the wild blue yonder once in a while. At least for now, I believe I may still rough it, hiking or camping. If eventually I were to be stricken down by some malady that even spending tens of thousands will not cure, I will face my demise with calm; with thoughts of having travelled where my heart once took me, feeling proud and content in my waning hours.

My body is an old car. I need to plan my journey carefully so that its remaining fuel will last to the end. In the infinite universe, life is ephemeral like the water lily that withers in no time. Before the inevitable demise, I must seize the moment, to travel, to see the vast land, to explore the glorious ruins left behind by other souls, other heroes of other times.

When people's minds are made up to go, many become obsessed with their checklists of the items for the road. They are amply illustrated in travel guides, too. If you are going to a colder region, you are advised to include leather gloves and snow boots. If it is the tropics, you are warned not to leave without sunscreen, sunglasses and insect repellent. Even to somewhere blessed with a moderate clime, you are urged to take a flashlight, Berberine tablets and the contact numbers of the embassy.

All these will come in handy of course. But one thing you must have with you each and every moment wherever you travel is your soul.

There is an ancient belief shared by an indigenous people in South America: they have to stop and wait for their souls to catch up if they have been moving too fast. Some will wait once every three days, and others once every seven days when journeying. In other words, they will not move ceaselessly. They need to be reunited with their souls that lag far behind. Our souls are like our spindly, ungrudging porter — they fall behind if we move too fast. This goes to show that our body and soul can be out of sync when we travel. But the consummate journey has to be one in which they are one, through thick and thin.

Good travel takes on a natural rhythm like breathing. To travel is to learn, and learning is a human instinct. Being a medical doctor once, I knew I must never stop learning. It has also become a habit of mine, even though I no longer work in the medical profession. Travel allows me to learn what all those who went before me had thought and done, how Nature had richly blessed and severely punished earthly beings, long before I came into this world. Travel makes one modest. You see majestic mountains, boundless oceans and how puny a place you occupy in the world. In travel, I learned that death is nothing to be sad about. Life never fades into nothing, but continues, only in a different form, in an endless cycle.

All this comes from the great affair of being on the move, from the divination of the soul. So, before you set out, remind yourself in a whisper to pack your soul, too. It is weightless and takes up zero space, but it is more important than a GPS device. It will be your sustenance; your bridge over a rivulet. It smiles when you are happy and weeps when you suffer. Even though it may not be the torch that lights up your path, it trails you faithfully, unflinchingly; never idling once every three days. If you travel without your soul, however, you are but a walking shadow; lifeless and hollow like the diversifolious poplar in the Gobi land that died centuries ago.

生命的借记卡

我有一个西式钱包，钱包里有很多小格子，这些格子的用途是装载各式各样的卡，我没让它们闲着，装得满满当当。我有附近多家超市的亲情卡，虽然我每次购物之后都毕恭毕敬地出示该店的卡，但一年下来累计的分数，总也到不了可以领取优惠券的地步（因为我购物不够专一，总是在各个不同的店家游荡），于是在某一个商家规定的日子里被残忍地"归零"，一切又要重新开始。

我还有电话卡，到外地出差的时候，虽然接待方会很热情地说，房间的长途已经开通，您只管用，

73

我还是为饭店附加在电话上的费用斤斤计较，出于为邀请方省些银两的考虑，自己到酒店大堂去打公用电话。每打一次，都有一种小小的成就感。我还有几家馆子的优惠卡，有次拿出来结账，服务员小姐看了半天，说不认识这卡，从来没见客人使过。我说，你来这家店多久了呢？她说，一年了。我说，这卡是你们店开张的时候给的，说是永久有效呢。小姐就拿了卡去问元老，笑吟吟地回来说，你说得不错，只是连她们也没见过这种卡，一直找到老板才说确有这么回事。

　　啰唆了这半天，还没说到正题上。我的正题是什么呢？就是我虽然有多张看起来也是硬邦邦闪烁烁的卡，但其实那种可以透支可以境外使用的货真价实的银行卡，一张也没有。先生说过很多次了，说这是时尚，你在高档场所结账的时候，如果掏出一大把皱皱巴巴的现金，是要遭人耻笑的。我说，你也不是不知道，我平日最频繁的交易场所就是农贸市场，别说那里没有刷卡的设备，即便有了，买上一个西瓜刷一次卡，买三条黄瓜半斤草莓再刷两次卡，你觉得如何呢？

　　家人就嘲讽我近乎一个纯粹的农妇，不能在金融方面与时俱进。好在这羞惭近日得到了雪洗的机会。单位为了发放工资方便，为大家统一办理了银行借记卡。

　　我拿到借记卡，反复端详并仔细地阅读了有关条文，突然思绪就飞到了很远的地方。

　　喜欢这个"借"字。我们的一切都是借来的，总归有要还的那一天。《红楼梦》里的公子贾宝玉出生的时候，嘴里是衔了一块玉的。我们每个人出生的时候，并非是两手空空，而是捏了一张生命的借记卡。

　　阳世通行的银行卡分有钻石卡白金卡等细则，生命的卡则一律平等，并不因了出身的高下和财富的多寡，就对持卡人厚此薄彼。

　　这张卡是风做的，是空气做的，透明、无形，却又无时无刻不在拂动着我们的羽毛。

　　在你的亲人还没有为你写下名字的时候，这张卡就已经毫不迟延地启动了业务。卡上存进了我们生命的总长度，它被分解成一分钟一分钟的时间，树木倾斜的阴影就是它轻轻的脚印了。

　　密码虽然在你的手里，储藏在生命借记卡的这个数字，你虽是主人，却无从知道。这是一个永恒的秘密，不到借记卡归零的时候，你在混沌中。也许，它很短暂呢，幸好我不知你不知，我们才能无忧无虑地生活着，懵然向前，支出着我们的时间，而在某一个早上那卡突然就不翼而飞，生命戛然停歇。

很多银行卡是可以透支的，甚至把透支当成一种福祉和诱饵，引领着我们超前消费，然而也温柔地收取了不菲的利息。而生命银行冷峻而傲慢，它可不搞这些花样，制度森严铁面无私。你存在账面上的数字，只会一天天一刻刻地义无反顾地减少，绝不会增多。也许将来随着医学的进步，能把两张卡拼成一张卡，现阶段绝无可能。以后也要看生命银行的脸色，如果它太觉尊严被冒犯和亵渎，只怕也难以操作。咱们今天就不再讨论。

也许有人会说，现在发布的生命预期表，人的寿命已经到了七八十岁的高龄，想起来，很是令人神往呢。如果把这些年头折算成分分秒秒，一年三百六十五天，一天二十四小时，一小时三千六百秒……按照我们能活八十年计算，卡上的时间共计是二十五亿二千二百八十八万秒（没找到计算器，老眼昏花地用笔算，反复演算了几遍，应该是准确的）。

真是一个天文数字，一下子呼吸也畅快起来，腰杆子也挺起来，每个人出生的时候，都是时间的大富翁。不过，且慢。既然算账，就要考虑周全。借记卡有一个名为"缴费通"的业务，可以代缴代扣。比如手机话费、小灵通话费、宽带上网费、水电费、图文电视费……呵呵，弹指间，你的必要消费就统统交付了。

生命也是有必要消费的。就在我们这一呼一吸之间，卡上的数字就要减掉若干秒了。我们有很多必不可少的支出，你必须要优先保证。首先，令人感到晦气的是——我们要把借记卡上大约三分之一的数额，支付给床板。床板是个哑巴，从来不会对你大叫大喊，可它索要最急，日日不息。你当然可以欠着床板的账，它假装敦厚，不动声色。一年两年甚至十年八年，它不威逼你，是个温柔的"黄世仁"。它的阴险在长久的沉默之后渐渐显露，它不动声色地无声无息地报复你，让你面色干枯发摇齿动，烦躁不安歇斯底里……它会让你乖乖地把欠着它的钱加倍偿还，如果它不满意，还会把还账的你拒之门外。倘若你欠它的太多了，一怒之下，也许它会彻底撕毁了你的借记卡，纷纷扬扬飘失一地，让"杨白劳"就此永远躺下。所以，两害相权取其轻吧，从长远计，你切不可以慢待了床板这个索债鬼，不管它多么笑容可掬，你每天都要按时还它时间。

你还要用大约三分之一的时间来吃饭、排泄、运动、交通、打电话，接吻、恋爱，到远方去旅游，听朋友讲过去的事情，当然也包括发脾气和生气，和上司吵架还有哭泣……当然你也可以将这些压缩到更少的时间，但你如果在这些方面太吝啬支出，你就变成了一架冰冷的机器，而不再是活生生的人。为了让我们的生命丰富多彩，这些支出你无法逃避。

当太老的时候，或者你太小的时候，你有一些时间将不知道自己是什么。当然，如果有另外的人清楚地记录着你的支出，我想那些时间应该被称为"成长"和"休养生息"。这是一些时间的黑洞，你却必不可少。就像你原来有一笔积蓄，你觉得自己很是俭省，从未乱花过一分钱，但那些钱财还是在不知不觉中流淌，让你囊中渐空。你幼小的时候不能工作和学习，这不是你的过错，只是你的过程。你年老的时候不能创造和奋斗，这也不是你的过错，而是你的必然。为了盛极时的响彻云天，蝉虫必须在泥土中蛰伏蜕变十五年，和它相比，人类还算早熟。人类的进步带来了人类的长寿，那多积攒出来的时间，基本上都是晚年。所以，你不能埋怨。你的生命借记卡上的时间的价值并不等值，对此你只有一笑了之。

借记卡有一个功能，就是代缴各种费用。你的生命刨去了这样多的必需支出，你还剩下多少黄金时段？

如果我们能够知道自己生命中能够有效利用的时间到底有多少，我相信一半以上的人都会活得更加精彩。因为借记卡的数字隐藏在无边的黑暗中，这就更需要我们在黑暗中坚定地摸索着前进。

你的密码只有你自己知道。不要把密码告诉陌生人，不要让他人主宰了你的生活。如果你的密码被泄漏，不要伤心，不要自暴自弃。密码是可以修改的，你可以重新夺回你对自己生命的控制权。这张借记卡，只要你自己不拱手相让，就没有任何人能把它从你手中夺走。

不要用你手中的卡，去做纯粹为了虚荣和炫耀的消费。因为那都是过眼烟云，你付出的是生命，收获的是荒凉。

不要用你手中的卡，去买你不喜欢的东西。生命是我们能够享有的唯一，它的光彩和价值就在于它独树一帜的意义。找寻你生命的脐带，它维系着你的历史和光荣，这是你的责任和勇敢所在。如果你逃避或是挥霍，你就彻头彻尾地对不起了一个人，让那个人在无望中泪水流淌。这个人不是你的爸爸妈妈，虽然他们也可能为此伤感，但在他们逝去之后，你依然可以看到新鲜的泪珠在闪耀。这个人也不是你的师长，虽然他们可能会因此失望，但他们还有更多的学生可以期待。要知道你最对不起的人就是你自己，你委屈了千载难逢的表达。

唯有我们不知道生命的长短，生命的价值才更凸显。也许，运动可以在我们的卡里增添一些跳动的数字？也许大病一场将剧烈地减少我们的存款？不知道。那么，在不知道自己有多少银两的时候，精打细算就不但是本能更是澄澈的智慧了。在不知道自己所要购买的愿景和器物，有着怎样的高远和昂贵，就一掷千金毅然付出，那才是真的猛士视金钱如粪土。

这张卡是朴素的，也是昂贵的。你可以在卡上镶上钻石，那就是你的眼泪和汗珠了。没有白金也没有黄金，如果一定要找到类似的东西，美化我们的借记卡，那只有骨骼的硬度和血液的温度了。

你的借记卡就是你的藏赘。当我们最后驾鹤西行的时候，能带走的唯一物品，是我们空空如也的借记卡。当那个时候，我们回首查询借记卡上一项项的支出，能够莞尔一笑，觉得每一笔支出都事出有因不得不花，并将这笑容实实在在地保持到虚无缥缈间，也就是灵魂的勋章了。

其实，当你吐出最后的呼吸之时，你的借记卡就铿锵粉碎了。但是，且慢，也许在那之后，有人愿意收藏你的借记卡，犹如收藏一枚古钱。

"Debit Card of Life"

I have a purse with many card slots, stuffed with loyalty cards issued by the grocery stores near my home. Although I dutifully present them at each purchase, I have never managed to accumulate enough points in any year to redeem coupons (perhaps because I shopped here and there, not being loyal enough to any particular store). Invariably my points would expire on designated dates and I had to start being loyal all over again.

Then, there are the calling cards. I use them when I travel. Although my hosting parties all kindly tell me that I am free to use the phone in my room for long distance calls, I worry about running up big phone bills and always used the public phone in the lobby to save some money for my host. I felt smug each time I had used my calling card for a call. I also carry a few restaurant discount cards. Once, I used one when paying my bill. The waitress, after examining its front and back, said she had never seen such a card.

"How long have you been working here?" I questioned her.

"About a year."

"I was given this when the restaurant was opened and was told it will never expire," I offered.

The girl took it to check with someone who had worked there the longest. "You were right," said she, smiling, after she came back. "The boss says you can use it, though none of my co-workers have seen it before."

I digressed. The point I wanted to make is that I never had a real bank card, the sort that you can use for payments when travelling overseas or for some cash advance, with all the shiny plastic cards I had in my purse. My hubby said that using a bank card is in, and that I could be laughed at for paying with a wad of crumpled banknotes at those posh places. "Well, you know full well that most of my purchases are at the local wet market. No vendors there have a card reader. Even if they did, who would bother to swipe a card back and forth for buying a watermelon here and three cucumbers or half a catty of strawberries there?"

I was roundly scoffed by my family for being like a farmwife and not keeping up with the times when it comes to money matters. Fortunately, I soon got a chance to wash away the shame when my employer arranged for us to each have a debit card for salary payment.

As I carefully read its terms of use, with the card in my hand, my thoughts drifted away all of a sudden ... .

The Chinese term for debit card contains the ideogram for borrowing (jie). So true! Everything we have is in essence borrowed and has to be returned one day. In the Chinese classic *A Dream of Red Mansions*, the protagonist Jia Baoyu was born with a jade pendant in his mouth. For us mortals, though we may be born empty-mouthed, we are not empty-handed. We are each born with a "debit card of life" clasped in our hands.

The usual bank cards are tiered, diamond or platinum cards being at the top. Yet the "debit card of life" is egalitarian, never discriminating against people by birth or wealth.

This "debit card of life" is transparent and formless, like the air that washes over us, like breezes that ruffle a bird's feather.

It is activated before you are even christened. Deposited into your account is the entirety of your life, quantified by the number of minutes and seconds. The slanted shadows of a growing tree are its footprints as it traverses time.

Although you have the password, you never know the exact number of minutes in your account — a secret kept until the very day of its expiration. Its validity can be rather short, which luckily no one knows in advance. So, we live headlong, without worry and fear, and spend freely, until one day the account is depleted and life comes to an abrupt end.

Many bank cards allow overdraft, both a benefit and bait, coaxing us to live beyond our means and politely dishing out penalties afterwards. However, the "bank of life" has no such gimmicks and its rules are strict and uncompromising. Whatever the deposit, your account diminishes by the minute and can never be replenished. Perhaps with future advances in medical science, one life may be linked with and extended by another. But it is not possible for now. Even if this were to be possible, it would be at the discretion of the "bank of life." If it feels offended or slighted, no permission will be granted — but this is a topic for another discussion.

Life expectancies are now in the seventies or eighties, as some may point out, which is indeed encouraging. If we convert the average life expectancy, say of eighty years, into seconds, then our "debit card of life" account can have a whopping two billion five hundred twenty-two million eight hundred eighty thousand seconds (Without a calculator handy, yours truly, though dim-sighted, actually worked out this huge number by hand and, checking it several times, believed to have got it right.)

It is indeed an astronomical figure. I breathed easy instantly, feeling puffed up. We all seem rich at birth, with time. But wait, there is more: we should take all into account while we are at it, crunching the numbers. We shouldn't forget the "auto-payments" that our "debit card of life" is set up for — amounts to be deducted in a flash without us even knowing it. For the real bank card, these may cover the bills for our mobile phone, home phone, broadband internet, utilities, and cable TV ... .

For the "debit card of life," numerous seconds are deducted for each moment we live. They are expenditures you simply cannot avoid and take precedence over others. To begin with, one third of your life has to be insipidly dedicated to sleeping. Your bed, unspeaking, unrelentingly demands your time each day. You may try to cut down the time you spend in slumber. You may do this for a couple of years or even close to a decade without having to pay for it. However, the revenge of the bed will come silently in the form of your gaunt complexion, thinning hair, loose teeth, restless temper and fits of hysteria. Even if you repent and pay fines, your cardholder status may still be revoked, and your account declared nullified. Thus, for your long-term welfare, you'd better get on with the demanding bed and give it the time that it is due.

Then you spend another third of your life eating, defecating, exercising, commuting, talking on the phone, kissing, falling in love, wandering in faraway places, listening to your friends' reminiscing, throwing temper tantrums, sulking, fighting with your boss, weeping... You can certainly try to cut down the time you spend on any of these. But if you are too sparing, you will look unanimated, wooden, not a feisty human. You can't skip all this if you want to live a colourful, fulfilled life.

You are not wholly sentient when you are too young or become really old. But should someone keep track of your account then, those years would probably be marked as "growth" and "recuperate" — the aurora and twilight of life that are indispensable. Life slips away without you knowing it, just as pennies saved frugally will eventually be gone. Playfulness in childhood is not a sin — it is part of growing up, nor is being unproductive in old age — a natural finale. Other than a raucous season of song at the peak of their lifecycle, periodic cicadas live as underground nymphs for up to fifteen years. By comparison, humans mature much earlier. Progress has also greatly extended human life expectancies. Yet, much of the prolonged human life falls in the waning years. The time deposited into our account is not of uniform value. Yet, it is something we can only brush aside with a smile. We shouldn't complain.

With all the time deducted by "auto-payments," what is left in our account of life?

I believe most of us would strive to live life to the full if we knew how much time we have at our disposal. As the exact amount in our "debit card of life" is hidden from us, we can only explore in the dark and find the path forward.

We should keep the password to our accounts safe and never tell any stranger, or else he or she will take control of your life. Should the password be stolen, don't throw up your hands and despair. You can always reset your password and take back control. If you don't voluntarily surrender your "debit card of life," no one can take it away from you.

Never use it on anything that only feeds your vanity and conceit. All glory and pride are fleeting. If you dispense your life in their pursuit, you end up in bleak desolation.

Nor should you use it for anything that doesn't truly agree with you. You only live once. The value and glory of your life lie in its uniqueness. Find the umbilical cord of your life — your lineage and history, which will give you a sense of duty and be the source of your courage. Should you shirk this responsibility and waste your life, you would have utterly let one person down. This person, teary-eyed and in despair, would be neither your parents, though they may also grieve, nor your mentor, though he or she can be disappointed. Our parents will eventually leave us and our mentors find others to goad, but the sorrow lingers, as you pass up the opportunity for manifesting your worth. For the person is no other than you.

Life is precious precisely because one is not foretold how long it will last. Perhaps exercise may beef up our account. Perhaps a malady may drastically reduce our savings. But no one knows for sure. Without a statement of our account standing, careful planning, instead of acting on impulse, is therefore imperative. Those who spend extravagantly, treating life as dirt, are hopelessly foolhardy, thanks to their ignorance of the cost of their aspirations and wants.

The "debit card of life" is plain but dear. It can be studded with diamonds — the crystalline beads of our sweat and tears. Yet in truth, it really cannot be described as such, not in terms of precious gems or metals. For it is made of our life and blood.

Such a card is our lifelong companion, our loyal Tibetan mastiff. When our hour of departure arrives, when life is finally at its end, it is perhaps the only thing we still have with us. A hint of a smile, real and lingering, after we have reviewed our account and found each expense purposeful and worthwhile, will be our ultimate reward — sweet laurels for our soul.

The worn card, the remains of our life, crumples up as we take our last breath. Still, someone somewhere may treasure it as a coin from antiquity, if it were to be found later.

人生有三件事不可俭省

无论世界变得如何奢华，我还是喜欢俭省。这已经变得和金钱没有很密切的关系，只是一个习惯。我这样说，实在是因为俭省的机会其实很多，俯拾即是、遍地滋生。比如不论牙膏管子多么丰满，你只能在牙刷毛上挤出一点五到二厘米长的膏条，而不是一米长，因为你用不了那么多，你不能把自己的嘴巴变成螃蟹聚会的洞穴。再比如无论你坐拥多少橱柜的衣服，当暑气蒸人的时候，你只能穿一件纯棉的T恤衫，如果把貂皮大衣捂在身上，轻则长满红肿热痛的痱毒，重了就会中暑倒地、一命呜呼。俭省比奢华要容易得多，是偷懒人的好伴侣——用最直截了当的方式和最小的代价直抵目标。

然而有三件事你不能俭省。

第一件事是学习。学习是需要费用的，就算圣人孔子，答疑解惑也要收干肉为礼。学习费用支出的时候，和买卖其他货物略有不同。你不知道究竟能得到多少知识，这不单决定于老师的水平，也决定于你自己的状态，这在某种情况下就有点"隔山买牛"的味道，甚至比股票的风险还大。谁也不能保证你在付出了学费之后一定能考上大学，你只能先期投入。机遇是牵着婚纱的小童，如果你不学习，新娘就永远不会出现在你人生的殿堂。

第二件事是旅游。每个人出生的时候都是蝌蚪，长大了都变作井底之蛙。这不是你的过错，只是你的局限，但你要想法弥补。要了解世界，必须到远方去。旅游是需要花钱的，这谁都知道。旅游的好处却不是一眼就能看到的，常常需要日积月累、潜移默化的蓄积。有人以为旅游只是照一些相片买一些小小的工艺品，其实不然。旅行让我们的身体感受到不同的风和水，我们的头脑也在不同风土人情的滋养下变得机敏，目光因此多彩，谈吐因此谦逊。

第三件事情是锻炼身体。原始人没有专门锻炼身体的习惯，饥一顿饱一顿全无赘肉。生存的需要逼得他们不停奔跑狩猎，闲暇的时候就装神弄鬼，在岩壁上凿画，在篝火边跳舞，都不是轻体力劳动，积攒不下多余的卡路里。社会进步了，物质丰富了，用不完的热量成了我们挥之不去的负担。于是要人为地在机器上跋涉，在残余氯的池子里浮沉，在人造的雪和冰面上打滚，在水泥峭壁上攀爬……这真是愚蠢的奢侈啊，可我们没有办法，只有不间断地投入金钱，操练羸弱的肌肉和骨骼，才能保持最起码的力量和最基本的敏捷。

有没有省钱的方法呢？其实也是有的。把人生当作课堂，向一切人学习，就省了上学的钱；徒步到远方去，就省了旅游的钱；不用任何健身器械，就在家里踢毽子、高抬腿、做广播体操……就省了健身的钱。

然而，这也是破费，因为我们付出了时间。

Three Things in Life You Shouldn't Skimp On

I love being frugal, however opulent the world has become. It has become a habit of life, having little to do with one's income. I see ways to be frugal everywhere I turn. Use a dab of toothpaste between 1.5 to 2 centimetres, rather than a huge blob, for example, when you brush your teeth. You don't need a lot, however plump the toothpaste tube is, unless you want to look like a mitten crab frothing copiously at the mouth. A cotton t-shirt may be all you need to be comfortable on a sweltering balmy day, however large your wardrobe. You don't need any fancy togs, lest you risk getting a heatstroke. Frugality simplifies things; good for those of us who just can't be bothered, allowing us to get to where we want to be on the cheap.

However, there are three things you shouldn't economize on.

The first is learning, which comes with a cost. Even the saintly Confucius demanded a gift of a bundle of dried meat from any prospective pupil. Yet, paying for education is somewhat different from that for merchandise. You are never sure how much you will get in return, which depends on both teaching and learning. Thus, it involves some conjecture, riskier than investing in a stock. For no one can guarantee that you will get your spot in college after paying for some courses. You have to keep your nose to the grindstone, or else a dream remains a dream, much like small children holding the bride's train fantasizing someday themselves walking down the aisle.

The second is travel. We are all hindered by

our limited experience and knowledge, like a frog sitting at the bottom of a well. Yet, we can certainly try to overcome our limitations, even though they are not our fault. To know the world, we should travel. Everyone knows travel costs money, but its benefits are not so obvious to all. Only over time do we see the positive effects travel wondrously produces — making us quick-witted, humbler and more insightful; with shining eyes and a mellow tone.

The third is exercise. None of the primitive peoples had a habit of taking physical exercises. Never being far from hunger, they were lean and without excess fat. As hunters pursuing prey, they became great runners out of necessity. They engaged in exuberant rituals, created cave paintings, and danced by campfires; all physically demanding. Only in the age of abundance, as a result of progress, have excess calories become a pervasive concern. So you see devotees spending hours daily on mechanized treadmills, bobbing in pools of chlorinated water, wallowing in artificial snow, skidding on manmade ice, or climbing cement rock cliffs. What extravagant folly! But we have no choice. We continue to pour in time and money to condition our muscles and bones so that we can maintain a modicum of strength and agility.

Are there any ways to save on these three things? In fact, there are. You can learn in the school of life, and learn from anyone that crosses your path, which will save you the expenses of learning in a building called the school. You can wander far away on foot, not having to pay for packaged tours. You can get all the exercise you need by shuttlecock kicking, knee lift, and rhythmic aerobics, without needing any fancy equipment ...

You will still be paying though; you are paying with your time.

幸福盲

若干年前，看过报道，西方某都市的报纸，面向社会征集"谁是世界上最幸福的人"这个题目的答案。来稿很踊跃，各界人士纷纷应答。报社组织了权威的评审团，在纷纭的答案中进行遴选和投票，最后得出了三个答案。因为众口难调意见无法统一，还保留了一个备选答案。按照投票者的多寡和权威们的表决，发布了"谁是世界上最幸福的人"的名单。记得大致顺序是这样的：

一，给病人做完了一例成功手术，目送病人出院的医生。

二，给孩子刚刚洗完澡，怀抱婴儿面带微笑的母亲。

三，在海滩上筑起了一座沙堡的顽童，望着自己的劳动成果。

备选的答案是：写完了小说最后一个字的作家。

消息入眼，我的第一个反应是仿佛被人在眼皮上抹了辣椒油，呛而且痛。继而十分怀疑它的真实性。这可能吗？不是什么人闲来无事，编造出来博人一笑的恶作剧吧？还有几分惶惑和恼怒，在心扉最深处，是震惊和不知所措。也许有人说，我没看出这则消息有什么不对头的啊！再说，这正是大多数人对幸福的理解，不是别有用心或是哗众取宠啊！是的是的，我都明白，可心中还是惶惶不安。当我静下心来，细细梳理思绪，才明白自己当时的反应，是一种深入骨髓的悲哀。原来我是一个幸福盲。

为什么呢？说来惭愧，答案中的四种情况，在某种程度上，我都一定程度地拥有了。我是一个母亲，给婴儿洗澡的事几乎是早年间每日的必修。我曾是一名医生，手起刀落，给很多病人做过手术，目送着治愈了的病人走出医院的大门的情形，也经历过无数次了。儿时调皮，虽然没在海滩上筑过繁复的沙堡（这大概和那个国家四面环水有关），但在附近建筑工地的沙堆上挖个洞穴藏个"宝贝"之类的工程，肯定是经手过了。另外，在看到上述消息的时候，我已发表过几篇作品，因此那个在备选答案中占据一席之地的"作家完成最后一字"之感，也有幸体验过了。

我集这几种公众认为幸福的状态于一身，可我不曾感到幸福，这真是莫名其妙而又痛彻心扉的事情。我发觉自己出了问题，不是小问题，是大问题。这个问题如果不解决，我所有的努力和奋斗，犹如沙上建塔。从最乐观的角度来说，即使是对别人有所帮助，但我本人依然是不开心的。我哀伤地承认，我是一个幸福盲。

我要改变这种情况。我要对自己的幸福负责。从那时起，我开始审视自己对于幸福的把握和感知，我训练自己对于幸福的敏感和享受，我像一个自幼被封闭在洞穴中的人，在七彩光线下学着辨析青草和艳花，朗月和白云。体会到了那些被黑暗囚禁的盲人，手术后一旦打开了遮眼的纱布时那份诧异和惊喜，那份东张西望的雀跃和喜极而泣的泪水，是多么自然而然的幸福。

哲人说过，生活中缺少的不是美，而是发现美的目光。让我们模仿一下他的话：生活中也不缺少幸福，只是缺少发现幸福的眼光。幸福盲如同色盲，把绚烂的世界还原成了模糊的黑白照片。拭亮你幸福的瞳孔吧，你会看到被潜藏被遮掩被蒙蔽被混淆的幸福，就如美人鱼一般从深海中升起，哺育着我们。

Blind to Happiness

A few years ago, I came across a survey conducted in a western country. A city newspaper asked its readers to nominate "The Happiest Persons in the World." Out of the entries by enthusiastic respondents, a jury of respected personalities set up by the paper picked the top three by voting, plus one more as a backup in case of any controversy. As I remember, "The Happiest Persons in the World" in the final list ranked by votes were:

1. A surgeon who has completed a successful operation, seeing his patient discharged from the hospital;

2. A mother holding a baby after giving it a bath;

3. A child smiling at the sandcastle that he has just built on the beach.

The backup choice was an author who has just put down the last word of his novel.

I felt stung when I first read this, as if by pepper spray. I doubted it was true and not some prank thought up by someone for a laugh. I was troubled and irksome and deep down was flustered and shocked. Some might say there is nothing outlandish or sensational about the survey at all, and that it is quite in line with most people's ideas about happiness. I agree. But still I felt troubled. I realized later after I mulled over my initial response that I was vexed by a profound sorrow, and that I had all along been so oblivious to happiness.

Why so? Well, to an extent, I had achieved what the top four happiest persons had done. I am a mother and bathing my child was once something I did daily. I had also been a doctor, having performed surgeries on many a patient and more than once seeing them happily walk out of the hospital door. I also had a playful childhood. Although I didn't build any sandcastles on the beach (the survey was probably done in an island country), but I did dig secret holes to hide my "treasures" in piles of sand near a construction site. By the time I came across the survey, I had already seen some of my stories in print and experienced the elation of "putting down the last word of my novel."

Yet, even though I had been through all four top-ranked states of happiness, I didn't really feel happy, which was very baffling and painful. There must be something seriously wrong with me. If I couldn't find the cause and have it dealt with, all my efforts and strife would amount to nothing more than building castles in the air. What I was doing might still help others but wouldn't make me a happy person. I was chagrined to realize I had been oblivious to happiness.

I wanted to change and take charge of my happiness. I began examining my perception and understanding of happiness, to enhance my sensitivity to and enjoyment of it. The sense of discovery was like that of learning to identify plants and flowers in their blinding display of colours, and of admiring the waxing moon and sailing clouds after being in a cave all one's life. I felt the delight, natural and ebullient, akin to that of a watery-eyed patient, eagerly looking around, after bandage removal following an eye surgery that freed him from eternal darkness.

An ancient sage once said, "Everything has beauty, but not everyone sees it." To parody him, we may say that happiness is everywhere, but some are blind to it. Being oblivious to happiness is like being colour blind — missing splendid hues in the world of colour around us. Sharpen your senses, so that you keenly feel happy — happiness erstwhile hidden or lost in confusion; happiness exhilarating, enriching, and rising from the depths like a mermaid.

心轻者上天堂

埃及国家博物馆有一件奇怪的展品：一方用精美白玉雕刻的匣子，大小约和常用的抽屉差不多，匣内被十字形玉栅栏隔成四个小格子，洁净通透。玉匣是在法老的木乃伊旁发现的，当时匣内空无一物。从所放位置看，匣子必是十分重要，可它是盛放什么东西用的？为什么要放在那里？寓意何在？谁都猜不出。这个谜在很长一段时间内，让考古学家们百思不得其解。后来，在埃及中部卢克索的帝王谷，卡尔维斯女王的墓室中，发现了一幅壁画，才破解了玉匣的秘密。

壁画上有一位威严的男子，正在操纵一架巨大的天平。天平的一端是砝码，另一端是一颗完整的心，这颗心是从一旁的玉匣子中取出的。埃及古老的文化传说中，有一位至高无上的美丽女性，名叫快乐女神。快乐女神的丈夫是明察秋毫的法官。每个人死后，心脏都要被快乐女神的丈夫拿去称量。如果一个人是欢快的，心的分量就很轻。女神的丈夫就判那颗羽毛般轻盈的心，引导着灵魂飞往天堂。如果那颗心很重，被诸多罪恶和烦恼填满皱褶，快乐女神的丈夫就判他下地狱，永远不得见天日。

原来，玉匣子是用来盛放人的心的。原来，心轻者可以上天堂。

自从知道了这个传说，我常常想，自己的心是轻还是重，恐怕等不及快乐女神的丈夫用一架天平来称量，那实在太晚了。呼吸已经停止，一生盖棺定论，任何修改都已没有空白处。我喜欢未雨绸缪，在我还能微笑和努力的时候，就把心上的累赘——摘掉。我不希图来世的天堂，只期待今生今世此时此刻朝着愉悦和幸福的方向前进。天堂不是目的地，只是一个让我们感到快乐自信的地方。

心灵如果披挂着旧日尘埃，好像浸满了深秋夜雨的蓑衣，湿冷沉暗。如何把水珠抖落，在朗空清风中晾干哀伤的往事？如何修复心理的划痕，让它重新熠熠闪亮一如海豚的皮肤，在前进中把阻力减到最小？如何在阳光下让心灵变得通透晶莹，仿佛古时贤臣比干的七窍玲珑心，忠诚正直诚恳聪慧，却不会招致悲剧的命运？

我们不是从一张白纸开始自己的心灵健康之旅。背负着个人的历史和集体的无意识，在文化的熏染中长大，它们对我们的影响复杂而深远，微妙而神秘。

如果你到医院检查身体，医生先要开出一系列的化验单，查验你的血，透视你的肺，必要的时候，还要把你送进冰冷幽暗的仪器中，用电脑拍摄你全身的照片……面对自己的心灵，也需先摸清情况，再对症下药。如何探知自己的心灵究竟是不是健康？这本小册子或许能帮你一个小忙（见《心灵七游戏》）。它收集了一些简单的心理游戏，每一个游戏我都曾饶有趣味地完成过。完成的过程中，不经意间就触动了心海下蛰伏的礁石，得以瞥见心灵深处缤纷的珊瑚和疾游的鲨鱼。中国有句老话，叫作"知己知彼，百战不殆"，你对自己多一分了解，你对未来就多一分把握。

有个广泛流传的说法，说是大脑皮层只开发了不到百分之五的空间，还有庞大的"哑区"没有被挖掘利用。当洗衣服的水都被节俭的人积攒起来冲刷地板的时候，我们怎能不善待自己的心灵资源？如果你渴求对自己有更多了解；如果你愁眉不展常怀戚戚并有愿改变；如果你希望自己变得更轻捷而有力，向着既定的目标迅跑；如果你顺风顺水还求更多的进步和欢乐，咱们一起来做游戏吧。书中的这些游戏曾经帮助过我，沉浸其中落下的泪水，已化作我的钻石。游戏完成时欢畅的笑声，已成为我生活中最新的习惯。游戏之后绵长的思索，更是多次帮助我在纷杂的世事中廓清方向轻装向前。

朋友，让我们一起来玩游戏吧。我和你分享这其中的甘苦，一如在沙漠的烈日中我们同饮一捧清凉的泉水，漫漫征途中我们合乘一车奔向远方。

Heaven for Light Hearts

On display in the National Museum of Egypt is an unusual exhibit: an intricately carved, white jade box, the size of a regular desk drawer. It was partitioned with translucent jade lattices. It was discovered lying empty next to a pharaonic mummy. Judging by the location, it must have been something of great importance. However, what was it used for? Why was it placed there? What did it signify? These questions puzzled archaeologists for a long time. The mystery was finally unravelled when a mural was found in the tomb of an Egyptian queen, in the Valley of the Queens at Luxor in central Egypt.

In that mural, a solemn man presides over an enormous

scale. In one tray is a feather while in the other a human heart that has been brought out of a jade box nearby. The judge of the deceased, husband of the sublimely beautiful goddess of joy, weighs the deceased's heart. If the dead man had been joyful, his heart will be lighter than the feather and his soul will ascend to heaven. If the heart is heavy, ridden with evil and sorrow, his soul will be condemned to the netherworld of eternal darkness.

So the jade box was used for storing people's hearts. Those who had died with a light heart could go to heaven.

After learning this myth, I have pondered on the folly of weighing one's heart upon death. It is just too late. When a person has stopped breathing, his life is cast in stone, making any attempt at remedy meaningless. I would rather prefer to pre-empt the final ill-judgement while I am still alive and kicking, by removing anything that can make my heart heavy. I do not aspire to a blissful ascent in the afterlife, but to being joyful and happy here and now. Heaven is not a destination, but a state of being buoyant and happy.

Your heart may be darkened by the detritus of the bygone; heavy and cold like a straw cape laden with late autumn rain. How can we shake off the rain and let the airy breeze wash away the pain? How do we patch up our wounded soul so that it glimmers, like the dolphin with its smooth, gleaming skin reducing the drag as it swims in the sea? How can our heart be light, with valour, candour and without shadow, like that of the ancient hero Bi Gan, but not repeating his tragic end?

In trying to achieve psychological wellbeing, none of us starts off with a clean slate. We all carry the baggage of our history and our collective subconscious, conditioned by our cultural traditions with their complex, profound, mysterious and enduring pull on us.

When you go to the hospital for a check-up, the doctor will first order a series of lab tests and a chest X-ray and, if necessary, full-body computed-tomography scans where you are fed into a cold, dimly-lit circular machine to have images taken ...

For your mental health, a sizing up before any treatment is also necessary. How do you make an assessment by yourself? I hope this little book *The Seven Games of Heart*, which contains simple psychological games, may be of help to you. I have tried each of them with great interest and amusement. While doing these exercises, I discovered things about myself which I hadn't known before, as if finding submerged reefs, or spotting corals of vibrant colours and sharks darting for their next meal. According to an ancient sage, "Know the enemy and know yourself; in a hundred battles you will not be in peril." The more you know yourself, the better your control of your own destiny.

There is a widely perpetuated myth that humans only use less than five percent of their cerebral cortices, with much of their brain power remaining untapped. With frugal people even reusing the rinse water from their washing to scrub the floor, how can we not make better use of our mental power? If you wish to know yourself better, to lift yourself from constant sorrows, to have a spring in your step, to move swiftly toward your goal, or simply to make more progress and be happy, let us try these exercises together. These games once benefited me and the lessons I learned are precious. I smiled more often by habit after I had completed these exercises. They helped me refocus on my goal and move forward in the humdrum of everyday life, unencumbered.

My dear friends: let us play these games together. The lessons that I offer will be refreshing, like the cool, bubbling spring water in the sun-scorched desert, and timely like a ride offered to a shared destination.

恰到好处的幸福

我喜欢"自拔"这个词，不是"跳"或是"爬"，而是"拔"——自己把自己拔出来。小时候玩过拔萝卜的游戏，那是要一群小朋友化装成动物，齐心合力才能完成的事业。现代人常常陷在各种情绪和成瘾的泥沼中，难以享受生活的美好，把自己从成瘾的伪幸福中拔出来，也是一个系统工程。

首先，要学会制怒。"怒"这个字，分成两部分，合在一起就是"奴隶之心"。如果你不是奴隶，而是奴隶的主人，你就有能力控制自己的愤怒，并使之渐渐平息下来，安定下来。而"定"是可以生出智慧来的，当一个人具备了智慧，他的处境就有了微明的亮光。

其次，也要适度担忧。担忧是永无止境的。人无远虑，必有近忧。适当的担忧是一种成熟与承受的能力，要不怎么古代的志士仁人都忧国忧民呢，但担忧过度就是愚蠢，不仅是子弹，让心灵也飞一会儿，正所谓放心去幸福。

最后，就是戒瘾。内啡肽这一强大的内分泌系统，正是我们得以感知幸福的物质基础。如果你不是有意识地、有智慧地支配自己的内分泌系统，它就按古老的遗传法则，在那里自行其是。有的时候是拔刀相助，有的时候则是完全倒行逆施，火上浇油。它都浑然不觉，没准还沾沾自喜呢。因此我们要学会和自己的内分泌系统对话，学会控制自己的荷尔蒙，这是新时代的新任务。

过犹不及，恰到好处，方得大幸福。

Happiness in Being Just About Right

I like the Chinese phrase "pulling oneself up." Back when I was small, we often played the game of "pulling the carrot," with everyone pretending to be bunnies and working together to extricate an imaginary carrot from someone's grip. The contemporary men and women are often mired in myriad emotional problems and obsessions, to the extent of not being able to enjoy life at all. To get oneself out of such a dire condition requires a three-fold effort.

First, one must learn to rein in anger. The Chinese ideogram for "anger" consists of two parts meaning "slave" and "heart." If you do not want to be "enslaved" by your heart, you should learn to control your temper and not let anger consume you. Calm leads to reason and wisdom, which makes change possible.

Second, put away excessive worries. People are inclined to worry endlessly. The paranoid pre-empt problems and are thus saved from being bothered by them later. It is a mark of maturity and fortitude. Our noble forebears, pillars of society with their place in history, worried about the nation's fate. However, to be a worry wart and fret excessively is folly. Give yourself a break, accept uncertainty and let it fly. Let your hair down and be happy.

Third, overcome your addiction. Endorphins, the powerful chemicals released by the body's endocrine system, give us the euphoric feeling. If the endocrine system is not wisely kept under control, with all its evolutionary flaws, it will function impulsively, producing positive effects sometimes while running amok at others. We must learn to interact with our body's endocrine system and control our own hormones. This is a challenge that we will all face in the new era.

Don't go over the top; aim for just about right, which is the sure way to happiness.

人心要有准则

别人不做你要求的事情，并不一定是因为他没有听懂你的话，他不跟从你，极有可能是因为他不想这么做。所以，你不必说了又说，那样除了把自己变得琐碎不堪，别无益处。这时候最好的方法，也许是让他自己去摸索，即使是头破血流，也是必须缴纳的滞纳金。

要学会拒绝而无内疚感，当我们拒绝他人的时候，常常容易引发强烈的内疚感，这会干扰决定。如果因为你的某个决定而伤害了某些人的利益，你不必内疚。内疚除了折磨自己，还会使人昏庸。

有时通往地狱的道路上，铺满了良好祝愿的地砖。这世界上悲惨的事情之一，就是善意成了悲剧的指路标。

有人把房子当成生活最好的原动力，这就像把金钱当成原动力一样，短视而荒唐。这两年房子涨价，人人都和房子有着千丝万缕的关联，房子俨然变成了家庭的一贤，甚至是太上皇。房子不像金钱看起来那么令人眼花缭乱，当我们想到房子的时候，很快就联想到亲情、温暖、团聚、会餐……这个速度快得让我们难以察觉，久而久之，很容易跨过房子的经济属性，直接进入到温情脉脉的氛围，以为房子就是家人和天伦之乐的代名词了。

唔，还是要分开。没有房子固然让人惆怅，但我们可以在租来的狭小房子里，享受人生的快乐，如果没有了心灵的对接，大的房子也有可能变成大溶洞一样空寥。

人生如果没有准则，一个有着丰富多样性和选择性的时代的降临，就是灾难。如同一条没有方向感的小舟遇到了东南西北风，你说它将驶往何处？物质太纷繁了，容易让人迷失。这不该谴责物质，只是要让心境更加清明。

Never Lose Your Principles

If you can't get others to honour your request, it is not that they are mistaken or defiant, but that they are unwilling. There is no point in repeating yourself, which does nothing but makes you look pesky and silly. The best is to let them explore on their own. They may stumble and fall, but it is all part of learning and its inevitable price.

Learn to say no without feeling guilty. Turning someone down can trigger a strong sense of guilt that deters further decisions. You shouldn't feel bad if you step on someone's toes when making the right decision. Don't be tormented by the sense of guilt. It only makes you look faint-hearted and fatuous.

The road to hell is sometimes paved with good intentions. It is one of the follies of humanity that good intentions sometimes lead to a tragic end.

For some, owning an apartment or house is their greatest motivation in life, as money is the same for others, which is absurd and short-sighted. As property prices skyrocketed in recent years, everyone seems to be ensnared — owning a piece of real estate becomes the overriding concern of each household. Property may not look as seductive and gaudy as banknotes. For when we talk about an apartment or house, we tend to think of family, the warmth of hearth, reunions and parties. Such associations are so strong and ingrained that "house" has become synonymous with family and the enjoyment of being with one's children.

Well, "house" and family are not equivalent. We can enjoy life living in rented digs, without owning an apartment or house. Likewise, without emotional bonds, a large house is no better than a empty subterranean cave.

Without principles and values, we would feel abysmally horrified in an era of diversity and dazzling choices; like a small vessel losing its bearing in shifting winds. When temptations are rife, we can easily get lost. We shouldn't complain that there are too many temptations. What we can do is to be clear-headed and sharp-minded.

用宽容治愈焦虑

宽容就是允许别人有判断和行动的自由。对不同于自己的观点和行为，哪怕已经预见到了一切危险的结局，也依然耐心地公正地等待。

这一点，好难啊。可能是当过临床心理学家的缘故，听过很多人的故事，知道很多人的结局，这也就让我的人生，在某种程度上记住了很多人的经验。我没有更精湛的远见卓识，只是像一只老啄木鸟，敲击的树干比较多了，对于哪里有虫子，判断力稍好。

最常有的悲哀，是看到危险渊薮，而当事人还以为是一马平川，逍遥向前。我大声疾呼警示危险，但人们闭目塞听优哉走去，令我惆怅叹息。时间久了，我也咽喉嘶哑，明知不可为而为之的耐心，渐渐消减。

更多的时候，因为当事人并没有征询我的意见，我也不能挺身而出干涉他人的生活，眼睁睁地看着列车出轨，人仰马翻。

人要想慈悲地输出智慧，不自作多情，也不是容易事。这种时刻，让我焦灼。

时间久了，也想明白了。不能以为焦虑不安就是贡献力量的一种方式，这是弄巧成拙，既帮不了别人，也毁了自己的欢愉。

焦虑本身并不是竭尽全力的表达，只是不良心理状态的折磨。其实，人生并没有一定的对错之分。生命是一个过程，万丈红尘、万千气象都是常态。宽容就是接受和自己不同的人生状态，并不歇斯底里。

Tolerance—a Cure for Anxiety

Tolerance means respect for others' freedom in action and judgement. We should give others their time, with patience and fairness, even if we foresee the perilous outcome of their views and actions.

This can indeed be tough. Being once a counselling psychologist, I have learned the experiences of many who shared their life stories with me. I don't claim any superior power of vision or insight. But I trust my judgement, like an old woodpecker that knows where to find the worms, having tapped many a tree.

I felt saddened to see my warnings ignored by those who,

on the brink of the abyss, thought blindly they were ambling into easy terrain. Hoarse as a crow, I'd find my patience wearing thin at length after appealing stubbornly in vain.

More often, I had my hands tied, absent of a voluntary request by the person in question and in turmoil, achingly watching him or her slide until they become a train wreck.

We are all eager to give our two pennies worth, out of compassion and self-importance. Having to hold off sometimes makes me feel skittish. However, I have learned over time that such anxiety helps no one and is conducive to nothing but ruining one's own joy.

Anxiety, an irrational and tenuous mental state, can be intensely tortuous. Life is a process and we should embrace it all, its ups and downs, joys and sorrows. Life shouldn't be judged simply as right or wrong. To be tolerant is to recognize lives different than ours have value, too, and to not be hysterical about it.

没有人是一座孤岛

生活是由无穷无尽的关系组成的。

你应该从中分辨出最重要的关系和相对次要的关系。比如你和食物的关系，就比你和小学同学的关系更密切。

食物是你每天都要和其发生关联的事物，它们要进入你的身体。小学同学，除了极个别的，都已成了回忆。

六十多年前，美国作家海明威说过：

"谁都不是一座孤岛，自成一体。任何人的死亡都使我有所缺损，因为我与人类难解难分。所以，千万不要去打听丧钟为谁而鸣，丧钟为你而鸣。"

　　人是一定要有一种联结感，这就是我们的命运。

　　每个人都与他人相联，断裂的时候才空旷无助。不过，不要失望，还会有新的联结发生，这就是自然法则。

No One Is an Island

Life is an infinite web of connections.

You should learn to determine which of them should have priority over others. For instance, your relationship with food is much closer than those with your primary school alumni.

Food is something you need and ingest daily. With rare exceptions, your primary school alumni exist in your memory only.

More than six decades ago, the American writer Ernest Hemingway cited this famous quote: "No man is an island entire of itself ... any man's death diminishes me, because I am involved in mankind. And therefore never send to know for whom the bell tolls; it tolls for thee."

Humanity has always thrived on such connectedness. Such is our fate.

We are all connected with others in some way. We feel helpless and small when such connections are broken. However, despair not, for new connections will inevitably grow. Such is the law of Nature.

逃避苦难

万里迢迢，到了甘肃敦煌。鸣沙山像一个橙黄色的诱惑，半明半暗卧在傍晚的戈壁上。

人们像朝圣似的扒下鞋袜，一步一滑地向沙顶爬去。

你是想后来居上吗？友人从五层楼高的沙坡上向我招手。

我抱着双肘，半仰着脸对她说，我不爬山。

那你怎么到达山那边如画的月牙泉？

雇一匹骆驼。

要是雇不到骆驼呢？友人从六层楼高的沙丘上

向我喊话。

那就只好沿着山根转过去。

这可是鸣沙山啊！友人已经到了七层楼高的沙峰。

不管是什么山，只要给我选择的自由，我就不爬。

我憎恶爬山！

我对友人喊，她已经到了十几层楼高的沙崖，没有回头。

她没有听到我的话，听到了也不会赞同。

经历是我们爱憎的最初的和永远的源泉。

我曾经穿行于世界上最高的峰峦与旷野，山给予我太多的苦难。那个时候我十七岁，当现在的女孩娇嗔地把这个年龄称为"花季"的时候，我正在昆仑山上度着永远的冬季。

在最冷的日子里，我们要爬很多皑皑的雪山。我背着枪支、弹药、十字箱、雨布、干粮、大头鞋、皮大衣，还有背包，加起来六七十斤。

第一天行进的路程，只是爬一座山。那座山悬挂在遥远的天际，像一匹白马的标本。

还没有走到山脚下，我就一步也迈不动了。宿营地在山的那边，遥远得如同我已死去了的曾祖父母。我完全不知道自己将怎样走过这漫长的征途。

缺氧使我憋闷得直想撕裂胸膛，把自己的心像一穗玉米那样扒出，晾晒在高原冰冷的阳光中。

　　生命给予我的全部功能都成了感受痛苦的容器，我的眼珠被冰雪冻住了，雪花像六角形的芒刺牢固地粘在眼皮上，绝不融化，眼睛像两只雪刺猬。呼呼的风声将耳膜压得像弓弦一样紧张，根本听不到除此以外的任何声响。关节里所有的滑液都被冻住了，每走一步都感觉到冰碴的摩擦。手指全然失掉知觉，感到手腕以下是光秃秃的……

　　时至夜半，我仍未走出那座山。我慢慢地、慢慢地倒向昆仑山万古不化的寒冰。我不走了，一步也不想走了，走比死亡可怕得多。枕着冰雪，仰望高海拔处才能见到的宝蓝色天空。我愿意永不复生。

　　参谋长几乎是用枪逼迫我站起来重新走。

　　从此，我惧怕爬山，仅次于死亡。

　　惧怕爬山，实际上是惧怕苦难。山，这些地球表面疙里疙瘩的赘物，驱使我们抵抗地心强大的引力，以自身微薄的力量把自己举起来。当我们悬浮在距海平面很远的山峦上，以为自己很高大，其实我们不过是山的玩偶。

　　苦难是对人的肉体和心灵的酷刑。那些叫嚷热爱苦难的人，我总怀疑他们未曾经历过刻骨铭心的苦难。或者曾将苦难与苦难换取的荣誉置于跷跷板的两头，他们发现荣誉飘扬在半空，遮蔽了苦难，他们觉得值。

苦难是对人的信念最残酷的锤打。当你饥肠辘辘，当你衣不蔽体，当你的尊严践踏于泥泞之中，当你纯洁的期冀被苦难蚀得千疮百孔之时，你对整个人类光明的企盼极有可能在这"黑海洋"中颠覆。命运之舟破碎了，只剩几块残骸，即使逃脱困厄的风口，理想也受到致命的一击。再要抬起翅膀，需要积蓄永远的力量……

经受苦难而不萎靡、不沦落、不摇尾乞怜、不柔若无骨、不娼不盗、不偷不抢、不失魂落魄、不死去活来，是天才、是领袖、是超人，非平常人可比。

然而历史是平常人创造的。

幸亏人类害怕苦难，人类才得以不断进步、发展、繁荣。假如人类什么都不怕，什么都满足，那么至今还穴居山顶、茹毛饮血、火种刀耕。

最稚嫩最敏感的部位最怕疼，例如我们的手指尖。粗糙它、磨砺它，指肚便会结出厚厚的茧子，这是一种悲哀的退化。

手指结茧可以消退，心灵的蛹若被苦难之丝围绕，善与美的蛾儿便难以飞出，多数窒息于黑暗之中。

当然，当苦难像飓风一样无以回避地迎面扑来时，我也会勇敢地迎上去，任沙砾打得遍体鳞伤，任头发像一面黑色的旗帜高高飘扬……

　　为了逃避苦难，我一生奋斗不息。

　　苦难也像幸福一样，分有许多层次，好像一条漫长的台阶。苦难宫殿里的至尊之王，是心灵的痛楚。

　　没有血迹，没有伤痕，假如心灵被洞穿，那伤口永世新鲜。

　　我相信在人类的心灵国度里，通行"痛苦守恒定律"。无论怎样的位极人臣，无论怎样的花团锦绣，无论怎样的二八佳丽，无论怎样的鹤发童颜，都有潜藏的伤口，淌着透明的血。

　　逃避了食不果腹、衣不蔽体的小苦难，便滋生出建功立业、壮志未酬的大痛苦，待功成名就、踌躇满志之时，又生出孤独寂寞、高处不胜寒的凄凉……人类只要存在感觉，苦难便像影子永远伴随。成功地逃避一次又一次苦难，人类就在进化的阶梯上匍匐向前了。

　　西域古道上，驼铃叮当。我骑着骆驼，绕到月牙泉。

　　没有爬上鸣沙山，你要后悔一辈子。友人气喘吁吁滑下沙丘对我说。

　　我不后悔。世界上的山是爬不完的，能少爬一座就少爬一座吧。

　　像逃避瘟疫一般，我逃避苦难。

Avoid Suffering

After a journey of thousands of kilometres, we were finally at Dunhuang, Gansu. The Singing Sands Dune towered over us in the Gobi twilight, alluring in its reddish glow.

People, after shedding their socks, were slogging up the slope of shifting sands, like barefoot pilgrims.

"Aren't you going to join me?" my friend called out way up on the slope, about five storeys above me.

Arms folded and gazing up, I shot back, "No, I am not going up this."

"How are you getting to the other side, for the Crescent Lake?"

"I will hire a camel," said I.

"What if there are no camels for hire?" she shot back, now perching six-storey high.

"Then I will walk."

"But this is the Singing Sands Dune!" She cried out, now on storey seven.

"Whatever! As long as I have a choice, I won't climb!"

"I hated climbing hills!" I hollered, in the direction of my friend who by then had gained the crest over a dozen storeys high. She did not hear me — nor did she look back.

She wouldn't have agreed, even if she had heard.

Our aversions and likings are rooted in and driven by our past experiences.

I had traversed the world's highest plateau, of towering peaks and vast empty expanse of snow. Mountains meant so much suffering, and high on the Kunlun, it was permanent winter for me, only seventeen then, an age when young girls are described nowadays as in their soft bloom of youth.

In the depth of winter, we climbed many a snow-capped

mountain. I carried a load of close to seventy lbs that included a rifle, ammunition, a medic's kit, tarp, dried-food rations, combat boots, shearling sheepskin overcoat, and a tactical backpack.

We spent a whole day on the first day of our march scaling a snowy peak, whose jagged whiteness floated high in the thin air like the mounted specimen of a white horse.

Before we even reached the base of the mountain, I was on my last legs, each step a struggle. But we would not stop until after our descent on the other side, which seemed so far away, as unfathomable as the nether regions where my long departed great grandparents were. I wasn't sure if I could make it to the end of the day's march.

In the thin air, I felt such an unbearable tightness in my chest that I almost wished I could tear my heart out and let it breathe in the cold highland sun.

My whole body was registering pain. My eyeballs felt as if they were frozen. Snowflakes, like hexagonal caltrops of ice, stuck to the eyelids; forming spiky icicles like raised porcupine quills. I sensed pressure on my ears in gusts of wind and could hear nothing but the ferocious howling. The synovial fluid in all my joints seemed to have frozen, too, as if there were icy bits in them crushing against each other with each step I took. I could feel nothing in my hands as if all the digits were gone.

By midnight, we were still not done with the mountain. I felt the pull from the abysmally eternal ice of the Kunlun Mountains. I stopped and didn't want to take another step. Climbing was worse than death! I wished I could just lie down and never wake up, head resting on the soft snow, gazing up at the clear sky — a dome of brilliant blue, the kind only seen on the highland.

My superior nearly pointed a gun to my head to get me to pull myself together and march on.

I have had a fear of climbing since, second only to that of death.

Such fear is an aversion to suffering. Mountains —
protrusions and warts on the face of the earth — force
us to defy gravity and haul ourselves high above and far
away from sea level. Though euphoric after scaling their
heights, we are but little gnats to the mountains.

Hardships torment our body and soul. I
have always doubted that those professing to love
hardships have actually experienced any searing
pain or real suffering. They may have treated them
as part of some bargain — after weighing them
against the lofty glory and honour they may gain in
return.

Suffering can also crush one's conviction.
When you are hungry and shivering in rags,
when your dignity is trampled on and held down
in the dirt, and when your innocent aspirations
are thwarted, your hope for mankind's future
dissipates in waves of dark despair. With ideals
crushed and future in doubt, it will indeed take

Herculean efforts, if one manages to escape the fate of doom at all, to spread one's wings again.

If you could endure tremendous hardships without wilting, degenerating, going rogue, plundering or robbing, being spineless, spiritless or hysterical, you are indeed a cut above mere mortals; a superhuman, the chosen, a leader of the pack.

However, history is made by ordinary people. It is the aversion to suffering that has brought us ceaseless progress, development and prosperity. Humans would have remained cavemen, hunter-gatherers, or slash-and-burn planters, if they had been content with what little they had, not being averse to suffering.

The pads of our fingertips are among the parts of our body that are most sensitive to pain. Sadly, their sensitivity can be blunted as calluses grow. You may make them disappear if you take care of your hands. Yet, if your heart is weighed down by sorrow and suffering, the goodness and beauty in you would be stifled, like silkworms dying in their cocoons in scalding water.

Of course, I do not yield when hardships befall like a sandstorm. I grit my teeth and stand tall, despite bruises all over, with my hair flying like black battle pennants.

I strive ceaselessly to break out from suffering.

Like happiness, suffering has ascending levels of intensity, a long flight of stairs. At the top stands the king of misery — the suffering of the soul. If one is heart-broken, a wound with no visible bleeding or scarring, the pain remains acute forever.

I like to imagine there is a law of "conservation of pain," which prevails in the kingdom of spirituality. Even the king of kings, or the beauties in their bloom of youth, or the most revered of elders, have experienced pain; with invisible wounds bleeding.

With suffering at the margins of subsistence well behind them, humans agonize over unfulfilled aspirations for success, achievement, and honour. When these are achieved, humans are then plagued by solitude and loneliness at the top. As long as humans have feelings, suffering is on their heels like a shadow. Humanity moves forward by continuously breaking out of suffering.

Eventually, I managed to get around to the Crescent Lake atop a camel; its bells ringing in the western desert all the while on a trail of yore.

"You will regret not climbing the Singing Sands Dune for the rest of your life!" My friend blurted, after skidding down the lee side of the dune, huffing and puffing.

No, I will not. There are more mountains in the world than you can ever climb. One hill avoided, one pain spared.

I avoid suffering like the plague.

无形容颜

除了蒙面匪，我们向人时都有一副容颜，或姣或陋，此乃上天与父母合谋的奉送。它像一件不是自主选定的商品，无处退换，不论满意与否都得义无反顾地佩戴下去，还需忍受它的褪色与破旧，直至与身俱灭。虽说整形与美容术可使某些乏善可陈的相貌得到修正，但从根本上讲，我们的脸都是造化随机奉送的礼物，绝非不喜欢就可轻易扒下，再换一张新的画片。

然而事情又有些怪异，按说千人千面，绝不雷同，但每逢分手之后，我追忆熟悉的朋友或新结识的诸色人等，他们的脸往往如淋了雨的泥娃娃，五官模糊成团，心头浮起的只是一汪暗影，好像柏油路上水渍洇开的油迹，朦胧浮动，难以界定。淡去的眉眼缩略简化成某种符号——亲切或是寒冷的感觉，温馨或是漠然的情致，和谐或是嘈杂的音调。或者干脆涌出一片颜色：柔润的夕阳红、华贵的荸荠紫、神秘的宇航灰或污浊的狗尾巴黄。更多的时候，一提到某个名字，与之相关的那张具体的脸仿佛突然被巨型"消字灵"涂掉，代之一股情绪的云雾，或愉悦或厌倦，弥漫心头。

早先以为自己有残缺，大脑里专管录像的那一部分遭了虫蛀，成了破包袱皮，再也包裹不住有关相貌的记忆，后来年事渐长，与人交流，才知天下有这等恍惚毛病的人颇不少。方明白人的脸，乃是一个变数。

眼光直接注视的时候，对方的眉目自然是清晰的。可惜心灵的感光，基本上是一次成像不保存底片，加上懒散，有形的面容一旦撤离视野，记忆就清理记录，大而化之地分门别类，一一归档。人的有形容貌，无法恒久烙下记忆，卷宗收留的只是提炼过的印象。

世上资产，分为有形和无形。无形资产的定义，我以为是指超出物质的实际价值，由于你的努力在人们心目中形成的信任——简言之，它是你的名字进入他人耳鼓时，呼唤起的一种美好感情。

摈除其中的商业因素，对于人的容颜来说，或可借用这个概念。

脸后有脸。

上天赋予我们的端正或歪斜的眉眼、粗糙或光滑的皮肤、颀长或粗短的身材、完整或残缺的四肢……均是我们有形的容颜，每个人后天创造发展的性格、品行、能力，属于你的无形容颜。

无形脸有正负之分。一个人只有美丽的外表，却没有相应的内在，初次结识时秀丽外形所留下的愉悦印象就会犹如沙上之塔，很快便会被残酷的现实冲刷得千疮百孔。无形容颜的毁灭，像一场"精神天花"，人际关系一旦被传染，犹如多米诺骨牌轰然倒塌。从此提起你的时候，人们会遗憾甚或恼怒地说："那个人啊，金玉其外、败絮其中。"

无形脸不会衰老。只要我们浇灌慧根、磨砺意志、拓展胸臆，它便会从幼年开始，如同花树一般渐渐生长，直至轮廓分明、明眸皓齿、青丝不老、慈眉善目……岁月流逝，沧海桑田，但在欢喜你、亲近你的眼光中，你所留下的形象始终如一，引起的感觉永恒温暖。比如远行的双亲，纵是白发苍苍，在儿女们心中依旧是盛年音容、风采卓然。

我们习惯以思为笔，在心灵之纸上勾勒众人容貌。它和古时衙门的"画影图形"不同，与真实的形象已无关联，只对真实的情感负责。无形容貌是想象和判断的产物，摒弃工笔，重在写意。它缥缈，却比纤毫不差的实照具有更持久的魅力。

　　无形脸可以美丽也可以丑陋，能怒火中烧也能垂头丧气，会神采奕奕也会惨淡无光。无形容颜的营造也像一门古老的手艺，"师父领进门，修行在个人"，如果你背信弃义，无形脸的画布上就留下贼眉鼠眼的一笔。如果你阿谀奉承，画布上就面色萎黄。如果你恃强凌弱，画布上就口眼歪斜。如果你居心叵测，画布上就血盆大口。如果你聪慧机警，画布上就眉清目秀。如果你襟怀坦荡，画布上就有浩然正气流注天庭。

　　我们对有形的容颜可以心平气和、随遇而安，对无形的容颜却要惨淡经营、精益求精。有形的容颜可以有疵而不坠青云之志，无形的容颜不能肮脏受污而无动于衷。

　　有形的脸可存在不完美，无形的脸必得常修炼。

　　珍惜每个人的无形脸，它是品德签发的通行证。凭着优雅的无形容颜，我们可以在萍水相逢的一瞬，遭遇千金难买的信任，转危为安；我们可以在旋转的大千世界，找到志同道合的朋友，共赴天涯。

Our "Intangible Face"

Our looks can be attractive or plain, a gift from our parents in connivance with the Creator, and are visible to all unless we are hooded robbers. Our looks are ours to keep and will wear and fade till they are gone with our demise. Whether we are happy with them or not, there is no return or exchange policy, like those for shop merchandise. A gift randomly given, our looks aren't something we can simply take off and replace, if we loathe them, even though cosmetics and surgery may amend some deficiency or blemishes.

Yet, although all human faces are distinctly different, those of my acquaintances, old or new, whom I had bid farewell to would become inexplicably blurred, like the smudged faces of clay figurines left out in the rain, when I tried to recall them. They were indefinable and shifting, like the sheen of oil on tar road surfaces. The once striking features faded into symbolic impressions: personable or cold, warm or aloof, cordial or blustery; or blended into patches of intense colour — mellowed red of sunset, imperial purple of the water-chestnut, mysterious grey of space missions, muddy russet of the bristle grass... More often, when a certain name was mentioned, my memory would be foggy and tinged with either delight or disdain; my mind blank, not being able to conjure up the face associated with it, as though it had been erased by disappearing ink.

At first, I thought I had some woeful mental deficiency. Perhaps the part of my brain that kept track of images was failing, like a sieve. As I grew older and talked to more people, I learned there were many who, like me, had dim memories of people's faces. It dawned on me that human faces can be intractable.

When we stare at a face, we have a clear picture of all its features. However, such a mental image is pitifully short-lived, unlike a photo negative that can be kept forever. Once the face slips out of our sight, it is processed and filed away in our memory, becoming a truncated impression, while the mental image is erased.

Assets can be tangible or intangible. To me, the value of intangible assets, beyond their material worth, lies in people's perception — the heartfelt trust that people have for them. Simply put, it is the positive emotion that their names elicit.

This applies also to the topic at hand: our looks — the "tangible face," and our inner quality — the "intangible face."

Our physical features — eyes, brows, skin tone, stature and four limbs, whether well proportioned, smooth, tall, capable or otherwise — form our "tangible face" and are a gift from the Creator. Our personality, character and ability behind our looks are our "intangible face," which we cultivate after birth.

One's "intangible face" can be either positive or vile. Yet, without inner qualities to match, pleasant first impressions thanks to one's looks can soon wane, the façade crumbling like a house of cards. If one betrays others' trust, one's relationships will all unravel. With the domino effect of failed trust, one's "intangible face" is blemished, as if scarred after the breaking-out of smallpox. People will lament or fume, "That chap is all talk and no show!"

Age will not wrinkle your "intangible face." It remains endearing, like an evergreen, flowering tree, despite the passage of time, if you can keep learning, keep building your character, keep an open mind and remain tolerant. As you age gracefully, people are drawn to you and dearly cherish the warmth of your glow. You are forever in your prime, like the beloved parents in the eyes of their children even though they are absent and have long gone grey.

Our minds are prone to capturing and cherishing what

strikes a chord in us — images of emotional truth, rather than mere representations — like the sketchy rendering, posted by the magistrate of old, of a suspect's face. The "intangible face" is a product of judgement and imagination, in a vein of impressionism; surreal yet more enduring than a realistic mug shot.

The "intangible face" can be beautiful or ugly, alight with rage or downcast, gleaming or glum. It needs cultivation, like a blank canvas to be filled with images of beauty by a practiced hand and by one's actions. If you have betrayed the trust of others, the "face" will take on a mean, crooked look. If you are obsequious, the complexion will be sallow. If you are a bully, the "face" will be scrunched up. If you are cooking up some evil scheme, the "face" will be mean and vicious. If you are smart and quick-witted, you are bright-eyed, and earnest of expression. If you are honest and open, your "face" will be the very expression of righteousness.

We must never cease perfecting our "intangible face," though we can be content with our looks. With imperfections in our appearance, we can still be optimistic, confident and hold lofty ideals. Yet, we should never tolerate imperfections in our "intangible face" and let ourselves lapse into mean-spirited thoughts and actions. We can live with blemishes in our appearance but must guard against the same in our character and conduct.

Let us take good care of our "intangible face." Our fine character, potent with virtue, is our passport to camaraderie and fellowship. With it, we gain instant trust in a chance encounter, getting ourselves timely out of harm's way. We find like-minded companions for our life's journey, amidst all sentient beings in the wide, wide world.

人生如带

人类送往太空的礼品中，有一盘录有声响的带子。

其他星球上的生物，有一天将凭着这带子认识我们地球人。

能在这样的带子上留下痕迹，该是至上的光荣。

人生的节奏越来越快。

好像有一只无形的狼犬追逐着我们，每个人都在和冥冥之中的某种速度竞赛。

有一个主宰一切的幽灵，拧紧我们的每一寸筋骨，驱使我们向前。

这是怎样一种至尊无上的力量？

它就是生命的不可重复性。

每个人诞生的时候，都是上天之手涂抹干净的一盘磁带。伴随我们的生命，它开始缓缓地转动，录下大自然的风雨，录下慈父母的教诲，录下前人心血的结晶，录下远方未知的问号……

在带子的尽头，是沙沙走动的无声无息的空白。

每个人都顽强地想留下属于自己的声音。

带子默然向前，不理睬人们的叹息与挽留。它只保存一代又一代人类最精彩的声响，使自身更臻完美与辉煌。

与人类永恒的传送带相比，我们每个人渺小如蚁、孱弱如丝、轻淡如烟、消逝如水。

带子输送着一代又一代的人们走进宇宙的深处，那是一去不复返的轨道。

带子不断清洗着嘈杂的声音，毫无商量地拒绝重复。带子只承认最新鲜、伟大的发明，在历史的沉积中变得越来越坚硬，要在上面留下痕迹越来越艰难了。

你必须用人类迄今为止最优异的养料滋润自己的头脑，你要站在巨人的肩膀上。

巨人屹立着，并不因为你的弱小而弯下臂膀。巨人沉默着，他们敞开自己，却不肯搀扶你。攀登巨人几乎费掉我们毕生的精力，许多人在这样的探索中凝固，成为巨人的一部分，悲哀地失去了自身。

当那些最勇敢、最智慧的人攀到前所未有的高度时，迎接他们的是严寒与荒凉。

面对纷繁的星空和遥远的黑洞，你踏出高贵而孤独的脚步。

你极可能走错，湮灭如灰尘。

带子是不保留探索者的脚印的，它淡然地看着一位位先驱者仆倒，只为成功者留下位置。

宇宙用死亡限制人们的步伐。人类的每一个婴儿降生，都是历史的一次重新开始。智者离开时，卷走了他们没有诉诸文字的所有发现。

历史不记录回声。人的生命是长度固定的锁链，为了对抗死亡，为了在重复学习之余留出创造的空间，只有在每一个生命之环上负载更多的希冀与沉重，人类日益变得匆忙与紧张。

做人是越来越累了。我们已无暇再创造语言与文字这类服务于全人类的精神奢侈品，我们已在忙乱中迷失最初的意愿。人们越来越频繁地聚散，物品越来越快地更迭。我们以为过程就是终极，我们在旋转，以为是前进。

带子沉默着。冷静甚至冷酷地等待着我们。

它只记录最优秀的声音。假如世间喑哑，它就耐心地等待。

人们在万籁寂静的深夜，倾听生命的磁带。

它均匀地无声地行进着，期待着。

The Phonograph of Life

A spacecraft on a voyage into the deep space carries a phonograph record. It was hoped that someday it would communicate to extraterrestrials a story of the world of humans on Earth.

It is a tremendous honour for anyone to be included in its selection of human sounds.

The pace of life is getting faster. Everyone seems to be racing against something, so frantic as if pursued by an invisible wolfhound. A sceptre prods us relentlessly forward, tightening its grip on all.

The sceptre is a force, primordial, that of life itself; neither repeatable nor replaceable, demanding its own fulfilment.

Each of us at birth is a phonograph record, having been wiped clean by the hand of the Creator, ready to be engraved as we move through life. It takes on sounds of Nature, such as those of winds and rain, naggings of our doting parents, messages of our forebears, and our questions about the unknown ... with faint cracklings in gaps of silence closer to the end.

We all wish to have our own sounds recorded. Yet sometimes the phonograph turns and turns, oblivious to our lamentation and yearning. Only the sublime sounds of ceaseless human strife are recorded and preserved through generations of self-improving humanity.

Against the background of eternal human strife, our individual endeavour is so insignificant, feeble, ephemeral and fleeting. The space voyager with the phonograph record is launched not toward any particular star and with no planned return trajectory.

But the individual recording of each of us is an ongoing enterprise. It filters out all the noises and repetitions, keeping only the remarkable, the breakthrough inventions. As time goes, the medium may age and become hardened. It will be increasingly difficult to engrave and leave any mark on it.

We see further by standing on the shoulders of giants, made wiser with the best of human knowledge accumulated over time. The giants, welcoming, will neither let us slip off their shoulders, because we are small and feeble, nor cradle us in their hands. We must learn to clamber up by ourselves, even though this may take a lifetime. Some sadly perish before they ever reach their perch, but they then become part of the giants.

The bravest and smartest, their efforts noble, face loneliness as they reach unprecedented heights, lofty regions of cold desolation, of distant stars and black holes. One single misstep, they are banished to oblivion, leaving no trace in the recording, which is reserved only for the successful, with no place for the fallen pioneers.

Death halts an individual's endeavour. Yet, each birth marks a new beginning. When the wise depart, all that is not recorded in words — their musings and discoveries — are gone with them.

History has no place for empty echoes. A person's life is finite; a chain of a set length. Death looms pressingly, and we resist death by our creative invention, with preciously little time left after the necessary learning and emulation earlier in our lives.

Increasingly, mankind is caught up in the frenetic hubbub of life. We become stressed, finding it hard to devote time and energy to creative activities using words and languages, which have become a luxury in the service of human spirituality. We have lost sight of our original goals, in the quickening gyration of gathering and departing, acquisitions and disposals. We are fooled into thinking that process is the end and that turning in circles is progress.

Our recording of life may become silent, having coldly and bluntly stopped registering the superfluous noises. For it is reserved for the sublime. It leaves a haunting void when the human world is all sound and fury, signifying nothing.

We listen to the recording of life in the quiet of the night as it rolls soundlessly ready for the true voices of life.

钱的极点

小时候猜一道智力题。问：从地球上的什么地方出发，无论往哪里走，都是朝向南？答案是：北极。

现在无论同谁聊天，无论从哪儿说起，都会很快谈到钱。钱成了当今社会的极点。

钱给人的好处是太多了，而且有许多人由于钱不多，而享受不到钱的好处。人对于得不到的东西就需要想象，想象的规律一般是将真实的事物美化。比如说，我们看到一位大眼睛戴口罩的女士，就会想她若摘了口罩，一定更是美丽动人。其实不然，口罩里很可能是一对龅牙，人家原是为了遮丑的。

我当过许多年的医生，虽是无钱之人，却凭医疗常识，想象钱的功能有限，理由是从人的生理结构而来。

钱能买来山珍海味，可再大的富豪也只有一个胃。一个胃的容积就那么大，至多装下两三斤的食物，外加一罐扎啤，也就物满为患了。你要是愣往里揣，轻则是慢性胃炎，重了就是急性胃扩张，后者还有生命危险呢。更不消说，长期的膏粱厚味，还会引起高胆固醇、糖尿病等疾病。所以说，那些因公而需长期大吃大喝的人，得了肥胖症，真是要算工伤的。

钱能买来绫罗绸缎。可再娇美的妇人也只有一副身段，一次只能向世人展现套在身体最外层的那套衣服。穿得太多了，就会焐出痱子。要是一天老换衣服，变成工作，就是时装模特儿了，和有钱人的初衷不符了。

再说人类延续种族愉悦自身的那个器官吧，更是严格遵循造物的规律，无论科学怎样进步，都不可能增补一套设备。假如无所节制，连原装的这一份都进入"绝对不应期"，且不用说那种种的秽病了。电线杆子的那些招贴纸，是救不了命的。

人和动物在结构上实在是大同小异，从翩飞的蝴蝶到一只最小的蚂蚁，都有腹腔和眼睛。人和动物的最大区别就在于思想，而恰恰在这一面钢铁盾牌面前，金钱折断了蜡做的矛头。

比如理想，比如爱情，比如自由……都是金钱的盲点。它们可以因金钱而卖出，却不会因金钱而买进。金钱只是单向的低矮的闸门，永远无法积聚起情感的洪峰。

　　造物给予人的躯体是有限的，作为补偿，造物还人以无垠的精神。人的躯体的每一个细微之部，都是很容易满足的。你主观上想不满足，造物也不允许你。造物以此来制约人对物质的欲望，鼓励思想的飞翔。于是人类在有了果腹的兽肉和蔽体的树叶之后，就开始创造语言、绘画和音乐……积蓄了一代又一代的精华，于是我们有了文学，有了艺术，有了哲学的探讨和对宇宙的访问……那都是永无穷尽的奥妙啊。只要人类存在一天，就会上天入地披肝沥胆地寻找与提炼。

　　我们现在是站在钱的极点上，但我们很快就会离开它。人们在新的一轮物质需要满足之后，回过头来仍然要皈依精神。

　　精神是人类最火的财富。在远没有金钱之前，人类就开始了精神的求索。人类最终也许将消灭金钱，但毫无疑问的是人类的精神永存。

Beyond Money~centric

A quiz I did back when I was a kid asks: From what location on the earth can you only travel south, whichever direction you take? The answer was: the North Pole.

Nowadays, in any casual conversation you have, the talk will inevitably careen to the question of money, as if it were some central premise of public discussions.

The benefits of money abound. Many are deprived of such benefits because of a lack of money. When something is beyond reach, speculation becomes rife, often with a glamorous twist. For instance, when we see a woman wearing a mask, showing only her attractive large eyes, we tend to imagine a beautiful face beneath the mask. However, she might actually be buck-toothed and the only reason for the mask is concealment.

I worked for many years as a physician. Though I never had a lot of money, I knew very well money's limitations, inferred from my knowledge of the human physiology.

Money can get you all the delicacies harvested from the forest and the sea, if you roll in it. Yet you only have one stomach. You'd soon feel packed to the rafters after tucking away large helpings, but two or three pounds at most, plus perhaps a beer. If you don't stop gobbling, you risk getting chronic gastritis, or worse, acute stomach dilatation, and death. Even if you are spared all that, with a rich, high-fat diet, you will inevitably have high cholesterol levels and become diabetic. For someone whose job involves a lot of wining and dining, food can be an occupational hazard.

Money can get you the best duds, but you only have one torso to put them on, however resplendent you are dying to be. It is only one outfit at a time that others will see. If you are decked out in layers on a balmy day, you risk getting an irksome heat rash. If you keep changing your outfits, you'd be thought a fashion model, contrary to your intentions.

As for the human organ responsible for procreation and carnal delight, it can't get away with not following the dictates of the Creator. No science and technology will give you a functional spare. Overdoing it may disable you temporarily, not to mention putting you at risk of all sorts of sickly ailments. Wonder potions advertised by charlatans on roadside lampposts won't actually save you.

By and large, humans are not that different from others in the animal kingdom. Even the dancing butterfly and the minuscule ant have eyes and abdomen. What sets humans apart is our power of thought — hence our spirituality. It is precisely this higher aspiration of ours that can help us foil the enticement of small green pieces of paper.

Money cannot buy ideal, love or freedom, though some may give up theirs for money. In this sense, money flows one way: it can only deplete, but not let you have more of, true happiness — the peak human feeling.

As our body is marred by physical limitations, we are compensated by the Creator with spirituality. Our bodily needs, in their regular puniness, are by design easily sated, however more you may yearn for. It is so that human desires for material possessions can be constrained and human imaginations soar. The early humans, feeding on game meat and clad in bark and leaves, began inventing language, painting and music. Through the evolution of their artistic creativity, we have literature, arts, philosophical discourses, space probe, and exploration of the unknown today. Such epic and arduous explorations will never cease, so long as humanity lives on.

Sooner or later, we will move beyond our

central focus on money — departing from the "polar centre of materialism." When the present universal drive for worldly achievements is once again played out, we will come full circle — with an abiding spiritual yearning.

Spirituality is humanity's greatest asset. Long before there was money, humans had begun their spiritual exploration. Humans may eventually evolve beyond money, and without doubt, the human spirit will endure and outlast all.

平安扣

女友送我一只翡翠平安扣，红丝绳系着。它通体碧绿，沉重地坠在我的胸口，澄清中透出云雾状的"棉"，水色迷蒙。扣的正中心有一个完整的孔，仿佛一支竹箫横断。清冽的空气在扣中穿行，染出一缕青黛。

我问友人，它是真的翡翠吗？

友人说，只是经过化学处理的石头而已。我把平安扣摘下来说，既然是假的，那还有什么意思呢？我看，这平安扣倒很像一枚铜钱。

朋友抚摸着平安扣说，它和铜钱实在是大不相同。铜钱外圆内方，上书"××通宝"的字样，内芯尖锐刻板，实在是锱铢必较之相。平安扣不着一字，外圈是圆的，象征着辽阔天地混沌无限，内圈也是圆的，祈愿我们内心的平宁安远。在它微小的空间里，蕴含了整个壮丽的大自然。它昭示当你的心与天地一致时，便有了伟大的包容与协调，锁定了你的平安。

我叹了口气说，讲得虽好，但世事维艰，我们脆弱的心，在历经沧桑之后，怎样才能清风朗月圆润如初？

友人陪着我叹气说，是啊！没人能承诺我们一生永远晴天，没人能预知草莽中潜藏着毒蛇，没人能勾勒出命运的风刀霜剑，没人能掐算出何时将至大限……从这个意义上讲，纵用尽天下翡翠，打凿出如泰山那般大的一枚巨型平安扣，悬挂在星辰间，也是没有丝毫用处的。然而，外界虽不能把握，内心却可以调适。任你弱水三千，我自谈笑风生，谁又能奈何我们呢？你我也许不知道，命运将在哪一个急转弯处跟踉跄跌倒，但我们确知，即使匍匐在地，也依然强韧地准备着爬起……

我把石头雕成的平安扣重又挂在颈上。

友人说，送你的翡翠是假，平安的祝福是真。每个人，都是自己的平安扣啊！

A Protection Charm

A girl friend of mine once gave me a green jade charm. Hung on a red braided silk necklace, it rests below my collarbone. Vividly translucent, it has a soft, cloudlike mottling of white. In the middle of it is a hole, perfectly round, like the cross-section of the musical instrument Xiao, with cool air flowing through it, weaving magic.

I asked my friend if it was real jadeite and was told it was just an ordinary, chemically-treated stone. I took off the pendant, doubting it had any use if it was not real jade. Instead of the enchanting Xiao, it now looked more like an antique coin.

"Well, it is different from an old coin," said my friend, gently rubbing the pendant with her fingers. "The old coin would have a square hole in the middle, ringed by four Chinese ideograms meaning 'universal currency' and the name of the dynasty when the coin was minted. The angular hole suggests stuffiness; something of a cold, hard-nosed bean counter. The charm, on the other hand, is plain, with a circular shape, implying the domed sky and its primeval vastness, and a smooth, round hole in the middle, indicating tranquillity and peace of heart. With the force of majestic nature encapsulated in its smallish form, it signifies peace, inclusion and equanimity when your inner world is in tune with the power of heaven and earth."

"It all sounded nice," I sighed. "However, how can we regain peace and keep the glow of our spirit undimmed, after going through all the trials and tribulations in life?"

My friend sighed with me, "True, no one can guarantee that our life will be all sunshine, without rainy days, or a jungle free of pythons. No one can predicate how destiny will toss and shape us, and when Death will fall with its inexorable decree. In this sense, no charm has the power to ward off all evils, be it of the choicest jadeite or otherwise, imbued with the force of Mount Tai and stars or not. Yet, even if we cannot harness all the external forces, we have the power to control our inner world. The truly brave are unruffled by challenges, however daunting they are. We may not know when fate will pull the rug from under us, but we struggle to get back on our feet whenever we are struck down. That much we are sure of."

I put the charm back on, one carved out of common stone. My friend said the simulation jade carries a genuine wish for peace and safety. In truth, we are all our own charms.